The Starlight Calendar...

Anonymous

The STARLIGHT Calendar

Compiled by KATE SANBORN

Alas for him who never sees
The stars shine through his cypress trees
WHITTIER

BOSTON AND NEW YORK
HOUGHTON, MIFFLIN & COMPANY
The Riverside Press, Cambridge
1898

To my Niece
MARY WEBSTER BABCOCK
who is not a "Memory," but
"more alive than the living"
to those who love her
I dedicate this collection of
proofs from all ages, countries, and
beliefs of the
Power of an Endless Life

Preface

SUNSHINE   RAINBOW   STARLIGHT
OPTIMISM   HOPE   IMMORTALITY

A natural sequence of titles, in my preparation of Calendars for daily cheer and consolation.

In youth, all are optimists. Farther on, optimism becomes a virtue; a grace to be cultivated.

When burdens bear heavily, and pitiless storms of sorrow beat on our heads, we must look up and find a Rainbow. Hope is then an essential for real happiness. At last, as the sunset shadows fall across the slope we are rapidly descending and night comes apace, we again look up, " through the cypress trees " to the stars, possibly inhabited, and to Him who made them, with positive faith in the life beyond. Seneca said, " The day of death is the birthday of eternity." You will find

Preface

blank pages at the end of the Calendar to record the sacred days on which your friends have passed through death to Life. We are all longing to meet our dear dead,—dead only in this world's ignorant phrasing.

> " The child who enters life comes not
>   With knowledge or intent,
> So we who enter death must go
>   As little children sent ;
> Nothing is known — but we believe
>   That God is overhead,
> And as life is to the living,
>   So death is to the dead."

KATE SANBORN.

January 1

Great songs of God are fast inclosed
    In the world-organ vast;
The winds sweep up the quivering pipes
    In stormy, angry blast.
But Faith sits at the keyboard
    And deftly strikes the keys.
'T is weird, 't is grand, how earthly reeds
    Breathe heavenly melodies.

Blow slow, blow fast, thou maddened blast,
    Thou shalt but Christ-songs bring
To trusting minds.   Blow, winter winds,
    Blow hard, — ye speed the Spring.
Wild hurricanes, the tender strains
    Of love Faith makes ye blow,
As though the angels strong and strange
    Hosannas flung below.
                    Denis Wortman, D. D.

There is always a Day Star in the skies.

January 2

Yes, it is true that there are moments when the flesh is nothing to me; when I feel and know the flesh to be the vision, — God and the Spiritual, the only real and true. Depend upon it, the Spiritual *is* the real : it belongs to one more than the hand and the foot. You may tell me that my hand and my foot are only imaginary symbols of my existence. I could believe you; but you never, never can convince me that the *I* is not an eternal Reality and that the Spiritual is not the true and real part of me. —*Tennyson.*

To destroy the ideas and hopes of immortality is to add death to death.

Madame de Souza.

January 3

The gift of God is Eternal Life, through Jesus Christ our Lord. — *Rom.* 6 : 23.

Death is as sweet as the flowers are. It is as blessed as a bird singing in Spring. I never hear of the death of any one that is ready to die that my heart does not sing like a harp. I am sorry for those who are left behind, but not for those who are gone before.

Beecher.

Can it be?
Matter immortal? and shall spirit die?
Above the nobler shall less noble rise?
Shall man alone for whom all else revives
No resurrection know? Shall man alone,
Imperial man, be sown in barren ground?
Less privileged than grain on which he feeds?

Young's Night Thoughts.

January 4

We do not believe immortality because we have proved it, but we forever try to prove it because we believe it. — *James Martineau.*

Gone into darkness, that full light
Of Friendship! past in sleep away
By night into the deeper night!
The deeper night? A clearer day
Than our poor twilight dawn on earth:
If night, what barren toil to be!
What life, so maimed by night, were worth
Our living out? Not mine to me,
Remembering all the golden hours
Now silent, and so many dead,
And him the last.

Tennyson.

January 5

For my own part, I have been long convinced that what we call death is a mere incident in life, perhaps scarcely a greater one than the occurrence of puberty, or the revolution which comes with any new emotion or influx of new knowledge. I am heterodox about sepulchres, and believe that no part of us will ever lie in a grave. I believe that the body of flesh is a mere husk which drops off at death, while the spiritual body — see St. Paul — emerges in glorious resurrection at once. I believe in an active human life beyond death as before it, an uninterrupted human life. I believe in no waiting in the grave, and in no vague effluence of spirit in a formless vapor. — *Mrs. Browning.*

That the spirits do not go far, and that they love us still, has grown to me surer and surer. — *Mrs. Browning.*

January 6

Call me not dead when I indeed have gone
Into the company of the ever-living
High and most glorious poets!   Let thanks-
      giving
Rather be made.   Say, " He at last hath won
Rest and release, converse supreme and wise,
Music and song, and light of immortal faces :
To-day, perhaps, wandering in starry places,
He hath met Keats and known him by his
      eyes ;
To-morrow (who can say ?) Shakspere may
      pass,
And our lost friend just catch one syllable
Of that three - centuries wit that kept so
      well, —
Or Milton, or Dante, looking on the grass,
Thinking of Beatrice, and listening still
To chanted hymns that sound from the hea-
      venly hill."

Richard Watson Gilder.

January 7

The incompleteness of the noblest part of man offers so strange a contrast to the perfection of the other work of creation that we are drawn to conclude that the human soul is only a bud to blossom out into full flower hereafter. No man has ever in his life reached the plenitude of moral strength and beauty of which nature gives promise. A garden wherein all the buds should perish before blooming would be more hideous than a desert, and such a garden is God's world if man dies forever when we see him no more.

Frances Power Cobbe.

All men's souls are immortal, but the souls of the righteous are both immortal and divine.

Socrates.

I believe and am firmly persuaded that a nature which contains so many things within itself cannot but be immortal. — *Cicero.*

January 8

I may say that I think I can see, as far as one can see in this twilight, that the nobler nature does not pass from its individuality when it passes out of this one life.

The life after death, Lightfoot and I agreed, is the cardinal point of Christianity. I believe that God reveals himself in every individual soul; and my idea of heaven is the perpetual ministry of one soul to another. — *Tennyson.*

Alas for the poor tale of goodness which age brings to the memory! There may be crowning acts of benevolence, shining here and there, but the margin of what has not been done is very broad. How weak and insignificant seems the story of life's goodness and profit when Death begins to slant his shadow upon our souls! How infinite in the comparison seems that eternal goodness which is crowned with mercy! How self vanishes, like a blasted thing, and only lives, if it lives at all, in the glow of that redeeming light which radiates from the Cross and the Throne!

Donald Mitchell.

January 9

Amid and above all the roar of the world, above the clash of the conflict in which we still have our part, they are speaking to us, as clearly and as sweetly as of old. They speak of their love for us, which cannot die. They speak of the love of God for us and for them, in which on earth they trusted, which now in heaven they fully know. They speak of Christ, of the joy of his service, of the glory of his presence, of the victory over death through Him. They speak of duty, and remind us how commanding it is. They speak of life, and remind us how brief and how rich it is. They speak of immortality, and bid us look upward and forward to it as our true home. Let us thank God for these voices that we hear, for these dear and sacred influences that come to us out of the unseen realms. A little while, and to us also the gates of pearl will open, and they who now speak to us out of the darkness will welcome us into the light. — *E. B. C. Coe.*

January 10

The soul, secured in her existence, smiles
  At the drawn dagger and defies its point.
The stars shall fade away, the sun himself
  Grow dim with age and nature sink in years;
But thou shalt flourish in immortal youth
  Unhurt amidst the war of elements,
The wrecks of matter and the crush of worlds.
                              Addison's Cato.

Not upon us or ours the solemn angel
        Hath evil wrought.
The funeral anthem is a glad evangel,
        The good die not.

God calls our loved ones, but we lose not
  wholly
        What He has given.
They live on earth in thought and deed as truly
        As in his heaven.

                              Whittier.

  The everlasting life is a present possession
continued into the eternal future.

January 11

The ghost in man, the ghost that once was
    man
  But cannot wholly free itself from man,
Are calling to each other through a dawn
    Stronger than earth has ever seen; the day
Is rending, and the voices of the day
    Are heard across the voices of the dark.
                     Tennyson.

    Yes, there are terrible costs in this world.
We get knowledge by losing what we hoped
for, and liberty by losing what we loved. But
this world is a fragment, or rather a segment,
and it will be rounded presently to our complete satisfaction.

    Not to doubt that, is the greatest bless-
ing it gives now. Death is as vain as life;
the common impression of it as false and as
absurd. A mere change of circumstances.
What more? And how near these spirits are,
how conscious, how full of active energy and
tender reminiscence, who shall dare to doubt?
For myself, I do not doubt at all. If I did,
I should be sitting here inexpressibly sad.
                     Mrs. Browning.

January 12

Man's unhappiness, as I construe, comes of his greatness : it is because there is an Infinite in him, which, with all his cunning, he cannot quite bury under the Finite. — *Carlyle.*

We must infer our destiny from the preparation. Everything is prospective, and man is to live hereafter. That the world is for his education is the only sane solution of the enigma. — *Emerson.*

How sweet, when nature claims repose
  And darkness floats in silence nigh,
To welcome in, at daylight's close,
  Those radiant troops that gem the sky!

To feel that unseen hands we clasp,
  While feet unheard are gathered round,
To know that we in faith may grasp
  Celestial guards from heavenly ground!

January 13

What we know as life is but existence,
  A waiting-place, a haven by the sea,
A little space amid immeasured distance, —
  A glimpse, a vista, of that life to be.
                      Chiero.

Whatsoever that be within us that feels, thinks, desires, and animates is something celestial, divine, and consequently imperishable. — *Aristotle.*

I feel my immortality o'ersweep all pains, all tears, all time, all fears, and peal into my ears this truth, — thou livest forever. — *Byron.*

The seed dies into a new life, and so does man. — *George Macdonald.*

Those who live in the Lord can never see each other for the last time. — *German motto.*

January 14

The spirit of man which God inspired cannot together perish with the corporeal clod.

Milton.

The thought of annihilation is horrible; even to conceive it is almost impossible. If we thirst for life and love eternal, it is likely that there are an eternal life and an eternal love to satisfy that craving.

F. W. Robertson.

Those who hope for no other life are dead even for this. — *Goethe.*

January 15

The more we sink into the infirmities of age the nearer we are to immortal youth.

Jeremy Collier.

What is human is immortal.

Bulwer-Lytton.

We are born for a higher destiny than that of earth; there is a realm where the rainbow never fades, where the stars will be spread before us like islands that slumber on the ocean, and where the beings that pass before us like shadows will stay in our presence forever. — *Bulwer-Lytton.*

That made me count less of the sorrows when I caught a glimpse of the sorrowless Eternity. — *Tennyson.*

January 16

That Science must and will prove Immortality is the message of to-day; for there is a distant and recognizable approach of the two worlds, the seen and the unseen, each of which is flashing its signals to the other.

Lilian Whiting.

I have no prejudice against a belief in a spiritual communion. If we are endowed with immortal souls, and preserve an individuality in another existence, it seems to me natural, judging by my own feeling of what I should be impelled to do, that spirits should desire to communicate with their friends on earth. The Bible teems with supernatural visitations, and if they are possible at one time, who shall say that they are impossible at another? — *Kate Field.*

January 17

They have passed beyond our vision, the
    loved and lost of earth,
They have gained the high fruition of hea-
    ven's second birth;
No longing turns their raptured eyes to earth's
    brief fevered day,
For life in rarest beauty shines untainted by
    decay.

They gaze upon their Father, 'mid the glories
    of his throne;
They are changed into his image, and know
    as they are known;
While his wondrous love grows grander
    within each pardoned soul,
As tides of lower ocean fill each inlet as they
    roll.

Around them throng the loved ones who be-
    fore them passed to light,
Whose graves made earth the lonelier, and
    dimmed its glory bright.
Oh, the rapture of the greeting where Death
    can never part!
Oh, the sweetness of reunion of loving heart
    to heart!

January 18

" The Power of an Endless Life,"—power to be, to achieve, to enjoy.

The wide universe the school, God our Saviour the teacher, and the pupil an unwearying and immortal mind. —*Rev. J. R. Berry.*

There may be beings, thinking beings, near or surrounding us, which we do not perceive, which we cannot imagine. We know very little, but in my opinion we know enough to hope for the immortality, the individual immortality, of the better part of man.

Sir Humphry Davy.

Cold in the dust this perished heart may lie;
But that which warmed it once shall never die.

Campbell.

January 19

The separation between earth and heaven is a narrow partition, and death is but the swinging of the door: the dead are living, more truly living than we. — *Lyman Abbott.*

Sometimes I think I am like a gardener who has planted the seed of some rare exotic. He watches as the two little points of green leaf first spring above the soil. He shifts it from soil to soil, from pot to pot. He waters it, saves it through thousands of mischiefs and accidents. He counts every leaf, and marks the strengthening of the stem till at last the blossom bud is fully formed. What curiosity, what eagerness, what expectation, what longing to see the mystery unfold in the new flower.

Just as the calyx begins to divide and a faint streak of color becomes visible, — lo! in one night the owner of the greenhouse sends and takes it away. He does not consult me. He gives me no warning. He silently takes it, and I look, but it is no more. Do I suppose He has destroyed the flower? Far from it; I know that He has taken it to his own garden. — *H. B. Stowe.*

January 20

I pray you for some little time not to muse too much upon your brother, even though such musings should be untinged with gloom, and should appear to make you happier. In the eternity where he now dwells, it has doubtless become of no importance to himself whether he died yesterday or a thousand years ago.

He is already at home in the Celestial City, more at home than ever he was in his mother's house. Then let us leave him there for the present, and, if the shadows and images of this fleeting time should interpose between us and him, let us not seek to drive them away, for they are sent of God.

Goethe thought it a sign of weakness to lose faith in Immortality, and said: "I hope that I shall never be so weak-minded as to let my belief in a future life be torn from me."

What God gives He gives forever.
James Freeman Clarke.

January 21

Beside the dead I knelt for prayer,
  And felt a presence as I prayed.
Lo, it was Jesus standing there !
  He smiled, " Be not afraid."

" Lord, thou hast conquered death, we know;
  Restore again to life," I said,
" This one who died an hour ago."
  He smiled, "She is not dead."

" Asleep, then, as thyself didst say,
  Yet thou canst lift the lids that keep
Her prisoned eyes from ours away."
  He smiled, " She doth not sleep."

" Yet our belovèd seem so far
  The while we yearn to feel them near,
Albeit with thee we trust they are."
  He smiled, " And I am here."

" Dear Lord, how shall we know that they
  Still walk unseen with us and thee,
Nor sleep nor wander far away ? "
  He smiled, " Abide in me."

Rossiter Raymond.

January 22

We must bear or we must die. The immortality of man disdains and rejects the thought, — the immortality of man, to which the æons are as hours or days.

All life is a school, a preparation, a purpose; nor can we pass current in a higher college if we do not undergo the tedium of education in this lower one.

Hast thou made all this for naught? Is all this trouble of life worth undergoing if we only end in our own corpse-coffins at last? If you allow a God, and God allows this strong instinct and universal yearning for another life, surely that is a presumption of its truth. We cannot give up the mighty hopes that make us men. — *Tennyson.*

January 23

As I stooped to kiss the lips of the beautiful boy, I knew, as well as man could know, that he was not dead; that He who had given more life to the daughter of Jairus and the widow's son had given it also to him; and that he had only gone farther upon his journey than I,—into a sweeter, fuller, more gracious life than he had ever known; and I also knew that I should see him again if I but made my own life as brave, unselfish, and true as his had been. —*L. Clarke Davis.*

The dust goes to its place and man to his own. It is then I feel my immortality. I look through the grave into heaven. I ask no miracle, no proof, no reasoning for me. I ask no risen dust to teach me immortality. I am conscious of eternal life. —*Theodore Parker.*

Not all the subtleties of metaphysics can make me doubt a moment of the immortality of the soul, and of a beneficent Providence. I believe it, I desire it, I hope it, and will defend it to my last breath. —*Rousseau.*

January 24

If the city of our heart is holy with the presence of a living Christ, then the dear dead will come to us, and we shall know they are not dead but living, and bless Him who has been their Redeemer, and rejoice in the work that they are doing for Him in his perfect world; and press on joyously toward our own redemption, not fearing even the grave, since by its side stands He whom we know and love, who has the keys of death and hell.

A living Christ, dear friends; the old, ever-new, ever-blessed truth. He liveth; He was dead; He is alive for evermore! O that everything dead and formal might go out of our creed, out of our life, out of our heart to-day! He is alive! Do you believe it? What are you dreary for, O mourner? What are you hesitating for, O worker? What are you fearing death for, O man? Oh, if we could only lift up our heads and live with Him; live new lives, high lives, lives of hope and love and holiness, to which death should be nothing but the breaking away of the last cloud, and the letting of life out to its completion!

Phillips Brooks.

January 25

The change has come and Helen sleeps, —
Not sleeps, but wakes to greater deeps
Of wisdom, glory, truth, and light
Than ever blessed her waking sight,
In this low, long, lethargic night,
    Worn out with strife
    Which men call life.

The change has come, and who would say
" I would it were not come to-day " ?
What were the respite till to-morrow,
Postponement of a certain sorrow,
From which each passing day would borrow.
    Let grief be dumb,
    The change has come.
                    Paul Lawrence Dunbar.

January 26

For does this soul within me, this spirit of thought and love and infinite desire, dissolve as well as the body? Has Nature, who quenches our bodily thirst, who rests our weariness and perpetually encourages us to endeavor onwards, prepared no food for this appetite of immortality? — *Leigh Hunt.*

How gloomy would be the mansions of the dead to him who did not know that he should never die, — that what now acts shall continue its agency and what now thinks shall think on forever! — *Johnson.*

Faith in the hereafter is as necessary for the intellectual as for the moral character, and to the man of letters as to the Christian; the present forms but the slightest portion of his existence. — *Southey.*

January 27

Immortality is the glorious discovery of Christianity. — *Channing*.

Truth, for Truth is Truth, he worshipt,
    being true as he was brave;
Good, for Good is Good, he follow'd, yet he
    look'd beyond the grave!
Truth for Truth, and Good for Good! The
    Good, the True, the Pure, the Just!
Take the charm "Forever" from them and
    they crumble into dust.

Tennyson.

All impatience of monotony, all weariness of best things even, are but signs of the eternity of our nature, the broken human fashions of the divine everlastingness.

George Macdonald.

January 28

Such a blow could not have been better borne than this has by all the family : no shutting up with grief; no hanging of the past with black, and making remembrance uncheerful; but such a state of mind as becomes those who look upon death as upon the entrance of a future life, who know that their sorrow is for themselves, not for him, and to whom the memory of the past remains a secure possession, sacred but not sad.

James Spedding.

The old, old fashion, death. Oh, thank God, all who see it, for that older fashion yet of Immortality. — *Dickens.*

January 29

What a strange moment that will be,
   My soul, how full of curiosity,
When, winged and ready for thy eternal flight,
   On the utmost verge of thy tottering clay,
Hovering and wishing longer stay,
     Thou shalt advance and have eternity in
       sight!
When just about to try that unknown sea, —
   What a strange moment that shall be!
                  John Norris.

John Stuart Mill, standing by his brother's dead body, said, " Here reason ends and faith begins."   But reason as well as faith teaches us that there must be a life beyond the grave in which the problems of this are solved, and seeming wrongs are shown to be truth and justice.

January 30

An old negro replied to a flippant young fellow who tried to convince him that there is no hereafter: "Dah's lots of work, sah, which I was made fit to do, dat I neber had de chance to do in dis worl'. I got de powers for it in my head, neber used. Jess like, when young mahs' go on journey, he pack all de clo'es he 'spects to use. De good Lord pack my trunk. He pack no clo'es but what I ken use — some time. De time 'll come to use dem, shuah."

Without a belief in personal immortality, religion is like an arch resting on one pillar, or like a bridge ending in an abyss.

Max Müller.

January 31

For half a century I have been writing my thoughts in prose, verse, history, philosophy, drama, romance, satire, ode, song, — I have tried all. But I feel I have not said the thousandth part of what is in me. When I go down to the grave I can say, like so many others, "I have finished my day's work," but I cannot say, "I have finished my life." My day's work will begin again the next morning. The tomb is not a blind alley: it is a thoroughfare. It closes in the twilight to open with the dawn. — *Victor Hugo.*

The eternal stars shine out as soon as it is dark enough. — *Thomas Carlyle.*

February 1

Tho' winds blow chill
   And snowflakes fall,
A Father's will
   Is over all.

Tho' hearts grow cold
   With pain and sorrow,
The promise old
   Brings glad to-morrow.

Not dead, not lost,
   Those gone before,
Tho', tempest-tost,
   Our hearts are sore.

As flowers of spring,
   They come again,
And bring clear shining
   After rain.

February 2

Never the spirit was born, the spirit will cease
    to be never;
Birthless and deathless and changeless remain-
    eth the spirit forever.
Death hath not touched it at all, dead though
    the house of it seems.
                 The Song Celestial.

My own dim life should teach me this,
    That life shall live for evermore;
Else earth is darkness at the core,
    And dust and ashes all that is.
What, then, were God to such as I?
                 Tennyson.

How can I cease to pray for thee?   Some-
    where
In God's great universe thou art to-day:
Can He not reach thee with his tender care?
    Can He not hear me when for thee I pray?
             Mrs. J. C. R. Dorr.

February 3

Our own are our own forever, God taketh
    not back his gift;
They may pass beyond our vision, but our
    souls shall find them out,
When the waiting is all accomplished, and
    the deathly shadows lift,
And glory is given for grieving, and the surety
    of God for doubt.

We may find the waiting bitter, and count the
    silence long:
God knoweth we are dust, and He pitieth our
    pain;
And when faith has grown to fullness and the
    silence changed to song,
We shall eat the fruit of patience and hunger
    not again.

So, sorrowing hearts who humbly in darkness
    and all alone
Sit missing the dear lost presence and the joy
    of a vanished day,
Be comforted with this message that our own
    are forever our own,
And God, who gave the gracious gift, He takes
    it never away.

February 4

Early wise and pure and true,
   Prince, whose father lived in you,
If you could speak would you not say,
   " I seem, but am not, far away " ?
Wherefore should your eyes be dim ?
   I am here again with him.
O Mother-Queen and weeping wife,
   The Death from which you mourn is Life.

Yet if the dead, as I have often felt, tho'
silent, be more living than the living, and
linger about the planet in which their earth
life was passed, — then they, while we are
lamenting that they are not at our side, may
still be with us ; and the husband, the daughter, and the son, lost by your Majesty, may
rejoice when the people shout the name of
their Queen. — *Tennyson.*

February 5

An argument for the continued existence of the soul when the body has been dissolved is the absence of correlation between the two. While they are united here, the body is the organ of the soul, and they are mutually dependent, each affected by the condition of the other. But the soul does not decay with the body. After middle life the body begins to grow weaker, but the soul still makes progress in knowledge, love, and power. In many cases the weakest body is the home of the most advancing soul. So it was with Schiller, Robert Hall, Dr. Channing, and many others. If the soul is simply the result of the body, this is inexplicable. — *James Freeman Clarke.*

I came from God and I am going back to God, and I won't have any gaps of death in the middle of my life. — *George Macdonald.*

February 6

Faith in God as Father and Friend of every child, such a faith as Jesus taught, gives us the greatest assurance of immortality. If earthly parents cannot bear to lose their children, and mourn over them while life lasts, shall the Universal Father allow his children to drop out of existence as soon as they are able to know Him and love Him? It is painful to us to cut down a tree which we have planted. Shall God cut down the whole human race which He has created?

James Freeman Clarke.

Through darkness and storm, and weariness of mind and of body, is there built a passage for his created ones to the gates of light.

Tennyson.

Death cannot claim the immortal mind;
Let earth close o'er its sacred trust,
But goodness dies not in the dust.

Sprague.

February 7

Three messengers to me from heaven came,
And said : " There is a deathless human
        soul, —
It is not lost, as is the fiery flame
That dies with the undistinguishing whole.
Ah, no : it separate is, distinct as God, —
Nor any more than He can it be killed ;
Then fearless give thy body to the clod,
For naught can quench the light that once it
        filled."

Three messengers, — the first was Human
        Love ;
The second voice came crying in the night,
With strange and awful music from above :
None who have heard that voice forget it
        quite ;
Birth is it named.   The third — oh, turn not
        pale ! —
'T was Death to the undying soul cried, Hail !

R. W. Gilder.

February 8

The most meagre sense of justice and right makes us conscious that man's earthly life is, morally regarded, only a fragment. Justice does not get accomplished. Conscience impels us to believe in certain moral sequences, but those sequences are seldom completed here. It is not that a future life is needed for compensation, but for the working-out of that moral completeness which the present seldom brings. — *Brooke Herford.*

I am gone before your face
   A moment's worth, a little space.
When you come where I have stepped,
   You will wonder why you wept;
You will learn, by true love taught,
   That here is all and there is naught.
He who died at Azan gave
   This to them who made his grave.
              Edwin Arnold.

February 9

Often together have we talked of death:
How sweet it were to see
All doubtful things made clear;
How sweet it were with powers
Such as the cherubim's
To view the depth of heaven.
O Edmund, thou hast first
Begun the travel of Eternity.
I look upon the stars,
And think that thou art there,
Unfettered as the thought that follows thee.
And we have often said how sweet it were
With unseen ministry of angel power
To watch the friends we loved.
Edmund, we did not err.
Sure I have felt thy presence! thou hast
 given
A birth to holy thought,
Hast kept me from the world unstained and
 pure.

Southey.

February 10

What is excellent, as God lives, is permanent;
Hearts are dust, hearts' loves remain;
Heart's love shall meet thee again.

Emerson.

Jesus Christ's career, taken all in all, is a photograph of humanity. He was born, suffered, worked, enjoyed, died and rose again. He "ever liveth." He becomes the argument (for immortality) incarnate or made visible. — *Rev. Emory J. Haynes.*

There is no end to the sky,
    And the stars are everywhere,
And time is eternity,
    And the here is over there;
For the common deeds of the common day
Are ringing bells in the far-away.

Henry Burton.

February 11

Not to the grave, not to the grave, my soul,
　Follow thy friend beloved.
　But in the lonely hour,
　But in the evening walk,
Think that he companies thy solitude;
　Think that he holds with thee
　Mysterious intercourse.
And though remembrance wake a tear,
　There will be joy in grief.

Southey.

Far off thou art, but ever nigh:
　I have thee still and I rejoice:
　I prosper, circled with thy voice;
I shall not lose thee though I die.

Tennyson.

February 12

They could not choose but trust
In that sure-footed mind's unfaltering skill
And supple-tempered will
That bent like perfect steel to spring again
      and thrust.
His was no lofty mountain-peak of mind,
Thrusting to thin air o'er our cloudy bars,
A sea-mark now, now lost in vapors blind;
Broad prairie rather, genial, level-lined,
Fruitful and friendly for all human kind,
Yet also nigh to heaven and loved of loftiest
      stars.
And often from that other world, on this
Some gleams from great souls gone before
      may shine,
To shed on struggling hearts a clearer bliss,
And clothe the Right with lustre more divine.
              J. R. Lowell.

February 13

I have for many years been often with the sick and dying, and I have never known a man to go out of life expressing doubts of a life to come. I have known men who during health expressed doubts of a hereafter. But invariably, so far as my observation extends, these men, as mortal strength ebbed away, let go their doubts and grew into the satisfying faith of an immortal life. At the last they were ready, without a doubt or fear or tear, to meet the marvelous change. It would seem as if the direct opposite must be the case if faith in a hereafter be a delusion.

A. J. Patterson.

Hope evermore and believe, O man ! for e'en
     as thy thought
So are the things that thou seest e'en as thy
     hope and belief.

Clough.

February 14

Weep not, my friends, rather rejoice with me :
   I shall not feel the pain, but shall be gone,
And you will have another friend in heaven.
Then start not at the creaking of the door
   Through which I pass.   I see what lies
      beyond it.

The grave itself is but a covered bridge,
Leading from light to light, through a brief
    darkness.

                    Longfellow.

If death were the exception and not the
rule, and we were not so swiftly to follow,
these separations would be intolerably sad.
We know no more of our next change of
life than we knew of this before we were
born into it; but that what we call death is
merely change, who can doubt ?

We shall follow and find them; all those
who belong to us. — *Longfellow.*

February 15

Of the immortality of the soul it appears to me that there can be little doubt, if we attend to the action of the mind for a moment : it is in perpetual activity. I used to doubt it, but reflection has taught me better. The stoics, Epictetus and Aurelius, call the present state " a soul which drags a carcass; " a heavy chain, to be sure, but all chains, being material, may be shaken off. How far our future life will be individual, or rather how far it will at all resemble our present existence, is another question ; but that the mind is eternal seems as probable as that the body is not so. Of course I here venture upon the question without recurring to revelation, which, however, is at least as rational a solution of it as any other. — *Byron.*

The tomb is not an endless night,
   It is a thoroughfare, — a way
That closes in a soft twilight,
   And opens in eternal day.

February 16

Life, we 've been long together,
Through pleasant and through cloudy wea-
   ther;
'T is hard to part when friends are dear —
Perhaps 't will cost a sigh, a tear;
Then steal away, give little warning,
Choose thine own time;
Say not Good Night, but in some brighter
   clime
Bid me Good Morning.

        Mrs. Barbauld.

For Life is ever Lord of Death,
And Love can never lose its own.

February 17

No; I shall pass into the Morning Land,
As now from sleep into the life of morn;
Life, the new life of the new world, unshorn
Of the swift brain, the executing hand;
See the dense darkness suddenly withdrawn,
As when Orion's sightless eyes discerned the
    dawn.

I shall behold it; I shall see the utter
Glory of sunrise heretofore unseen,
Freshening the woodland ways with brighter
    green,
And calling into life all wings that flutter,
All throats of music and all eyes of light,
And driving o'er the verge the intolerable
    night.

Mortimer Collins.

O change! O wondrous change!
    Burst are the prison bars.
This moment there so low,
So agonized — and now
    Beyond the stars.

Caroline Bowles Southey.

February 18

Death but entombs the body, life the soul.

. . . .

Death is the crown of life :
Were death denied, even fools would wish to
      die.
Death wounds to cure : we fall ; we reign ;
Spring from our fetters, fasten in the skies ;
Where blooming Eden withers in our sight :
Death gives us more than was in Eden lost.
This king of terrors is the prince of peace.
When shall I die? When shall I live for-
      ever ?

Young.

How gloomy would be the mansions of the
dead to him who did not know that he should
never die ; that what now acts shall continue
its agency, and what now thinks shall think
on forever ! — *John Fiske.*

February 19

We carry the image of God in us, — a rational and immortal soul; and though we be now miserable and feeble, yet we aspire after eternal happiness and finally expect a great exaltation of all our natural powers. — *Bentley.*

Our birth is but a sleep and a forgetting :
    The soul that rises with us, our life's star,
Hath had elsewhere its setting,
    And cometh from afar :

Hence, in a season of calm weather,
    Though inland far we be,
Our souls have sight of that immortal sea
    Which brought us hither.

Wordsworth.

You see no light beyond the stars,
No hope of lasting joys to come?
I feel, thank God, no narrow bars
Between me and my final home.
James T. Fields.

Shall I be left forgotten in the dust,
When Fate relenting lets the flowers revive?
Shall Nature's voice, to man alone unjust,
Bid him, though doomed to perish, hope to
live?
Is it for this fair Virtue oft must strive
With disappointment, penury, and pain?
No; Heaven's immortal spring shall yet
arrive,
And man's majestic beauty bloom again,
Bright through the eternal year of Love's tri-
umphant reign.
James Beattie.

February 21

A gentle waking to a newer beauty,
A gradual unfolding to the soul life,
As though a rose's chrysalid transported
Into the blooming valley of that Eden;
A slow unfolding of that early blossom;
A little kneeling at the sapphire portals,
And consciousness of all surcease of heartache,
Tumultuous tremor as the soul receiveth
The grander splendor of the spheral chorus,
That joy which passeth human understand-
      ing, —
This is that coming of that other morning,
This is that morning of the life immortal.
Frederick Peterson.

    Death's truer name
Is Onward: no discordance in the roll
And march of that Eternal Harmony
Whereto the worlds beat time.
Tennyson.

February 22

Death is the opening of a more subtle life. In the flower, it sets free the perfume; in the chrysalis, the butterfly; in man, the soul.

Juliette Adam.

With patriotic pride, we review the life of our Washington, and compare him with those of other countries who have been preëminent in fame. Ancient and modern times are diminished before him. . . Such was the man whom we deplore. Thanks to God, his glory is consummated. Washington yet lives on earth in his spotless example; his spirit is in heaven.

Letter from the Senate to President Adams.

This world is not conclusion,
  A sequel lies beyond,
Invisible as music,
  But positive as sound.

Emily Dickinson.

February 23

As in a wheel, all sinks, to reascend,
Emblems of man, who passes, not expires;
With this minute distinction, emblems just,
Nature revolves, but man advances, both
Eternal; that a circle, this a line;
That gravitates, this soars.   The aspiring soul,
Ardent and tremulous, like flame ascends,
Zeal and humility her wings, to heaven.
The world of matter, with its various forms,
Dies into new life.   Life born from death
Rolls the vast mass, and shall forever roll;
No single atom, once in being, lost.
                                        Young.

Decay alone decays;
A moment — death's dull sleep is o'er; and we
Drink the immortal air.
                                  Mortimer Collins.

February 24

1. The persistent and universal belief in a hereafter.

2. The consciousness that we are something somehow different and other than the body which we inhabit and which must die.

3. The continuity of our personality. The body continually changes. We remain.

4. The fact that man does not here reach manifestly the full development of his powers.

5. The ethical reason. The balances do not swing evenly here. They must somewhere, or all our sense of right and wrong is a deception.

6. The great reason is the resurrection of the Lord Jesus. This is the impregnable reason.

Wayland Hoyt, " Proofs of Immortality."

February 25

How inexhaustibly the spirit grows!
One object she seemed erewhile born to reach
With her whole energies and die content,
So like a wall at the world's end it stood,
With naught beyond to live for: is it reached?
Already are new, undreamed energies
Outgrowing under and extending further
To a new object: there's another world!

Browning.

And thus I know this earth is not my sphere,
For I cannot so narrow me but that I still
      exceed it.

Browning.

February 26

I doubt whether I can bring you any solace, except indeed by stating my own belief that the son whom you loved is not really what we call dead, but more actually living than when alive here. You cannot catch the voice, or feel the hands, or kiss the cheek, that is all; a separation for an hour, not an eternal farewell. If it were not so, that which made us would seem too cruel a power to be worshiped and could not be loved; but I trust you believe all this, and by this time have attained to some degree of tranquillity. — *Tennyson.*

For what is our proof of immortality? Not the analogies of nature, — the resurrection of nature from a winter grave, or the emancipation of the butterfly. Not even the testimony to the fact of risen dead; for who does not know how shadowy and unsubstantial these intellectual proofs become in unspiritual frames of mind? No; the life of the spirit is the evidence. Heaven begun, is the living proof that makes the heaven to come credible.

John Ruskin.

February 27

Yet Love will dream and Faith will trust,
Since He who knows our need is just,
That somewhere, somehow, meet we must.
Alas for him who never sees
The stars shine through his cypress-trees;
Who hopeless lays his dead away,
Nor looks to see the breaking day
Across the mournful marbles play;
Who hath not·learned, in hours of faith,
The truth to flesh and sense unknown,
That life is ever lord of death,
And love can never lose its own!

Whittier.

Faithful friends!   It lies, I know,
Pale and white and cold as snow;
And ye say, Abdallah 's dead,
Weeping at the feet and head.
I can see your falling tears,
I can hear your sighs and prayers;
Yet I smile and whisper this, —
I am not the thing you kiss;
Cease your tears and let it lie;
It was mine, it is not I.

Arnold.

February 28

I have a house, a closet which holds my books, a stable, a garden, a field; are these, any or all, a reason for refusing the angel who beckons me away, as if there were no room or skylight elsewhere that could produce for me what my wants require? — *Emerson.*

I am a better believer in, and all serious souls are better believers in, immortality than we can give grounds for. The real evidence is too subtle, or is higher than we can write down in propositions. We cannot prove our faith by syllogisms. — *Emerson.*

Ye stars that are the poetry of heaven.
Lord Byron.

February 29

At end of love, at end of life,
At end of joy, at end of strife,
At end of all we cling to so,
The sun is setting.   Must we go?

At dawn of love, at dawn of life,
At dawn of peace that follows strife,
At dawn of all we long for so,
The sun is rising; let us go.

Now I am entering the quiet harbor.
There has been much that was dark and hard
to understand; there is much still: but there
is plenty to prove that my heavenly Father
is leading me home as a little child.

E. P. Roe.

March 1

When rosy plumelets tuft the larch,
   And rarely pipes the mounted thrush,
   Or, underneath the barren bush,
Flits by the sea-blue bird of March, —

Come, wear the form by which I know
   Thy spirit in time among thy peers;
   The hope of unaccomplished years
Be large and lucid round thy brow.

Come, not in watches of the night,
   But where the sunbeam broodeth warm,
   Come beauteous in thine after form,
And like a finer light in light.   •

Tennyson.

March 2

For what to us seems dying
    Is but another birth,
A spirit upward flying
    From the broken shell of earth.

Heaven is not far. We are like phials of water in the midst of the ocean. Eternity, heaven, God, are all around us, and we are full of God. Let the thin crystal break and it is all one. — *Father Taylor*.

"Look at me," said the bubbling spring. "The black ice shut me in, as the black earth will cover your mother, but it did not hurt me; and, sparkling again this morning as brightly as ever, I am here to comfort you."

March 3

I believe we shall in some manner be cherished by our Maker, — that the One who gave us this remarkable earth has the power and will further to surprise that which He has caused.

A letter always feels to me like Immortality, because it is the mind alone without corporeal frame.

How brittle are the piers
    On which our faith doth tread!
No bridge below doth totter so,
    Yet none hath such a crowd.

It is as old as God;
    Indeed 't was built by Him.
He sent his Son to test the plank,
    And He pronounced it firm.
Emily Dickinson.

March 4

Dear, beauteous death, the jewel of the just,
    Shining nowhere but in the dark;
What mysteries do lie beyond thy dust,
    Could man outlook that mark!

He that hath found some fledged bird's nest
        may know
    At first sight if the bird be flown;
But what fair dell or grove he sings in now,
    That is to him unknown.

And yet, as angels, in some brighter dreams,
    Call to the soul when man doth sleep,
So some strange thoughts transcend our
        wonted themes,
    And into glory peep.
                 Henry Vaughan.

March 5

The rising of Jesus is still the source of comfort to thousands of broken hearts. As we look up, we see the heavens opened; but when we look down, we see only the earth. Fully to believe in immortality we must live an immortal life. Then the eternal life abides in us. Then all things are ours, whether life or death, or things present or things to come; or, as Dr. Channing once said, "Immortality begins here." — *James Freeman Clarke.*

"Listen to us," said the birds over her head. "We did not sing here last winter, but we were singing where the cold winds never blow. So your mother has only flown away to a sunnier clime, and we are here to comfort you." — *E. P. Roe.*

March 6

In my judgment, the most reasonable view that can be entertained, the view that explains most, leaves least unexplained, and provides for complete explanation at last, is that the universe has a Creator and Sustainer, this world has a Ruler and Lord, the nations of the earth a Governor and Judge, and men individually everywhere a heavenly Father and Friend. My strongest proof of immortality, therefore, is that it is an essential part of this order of thought; that it is bound up with this interpretation of the world's life, that of necessity it belongs to this philosophy of the universe. — *Geo. A. Gordon.*

Ah! on the brink
Of each new age of great eternity, I think,
　After the ages have all countless grown,
Our souls will poise and launch with eager
　　　wing,
　Forgetting blessedness, already known,
In sweet impatience for God's next good
　　　thing!

H. H.

March 7

There is no death!   The stars go down
   To rise upon some fairer shore;
And bright in Heaven's jeweled crown
   They shine for evermore.

There is no death!   The dust we tread
   Shall change beneath the summer showers
To golden grain and mellow fruit
   Or rainbow-tinted flowers.

There is no death!   The leaves may fall,
   The flowers may fade and pass away:
They only wait, through wintry showers,
   The coming of the May.

March 8

There is no death!   An angel form
   Walks o'er the earth with silent tread:
He bears the best-beloved away,
   And then we call them "dead."

Born into that undying life,
   They leave us but to come again:
With joy we welcome them, — the same
   Except for sin and pain.

And ever near us, though unseen,
   The dear, immortal spirits tread;
For all the boundless universe
   Is life — there are no dead.

March 9

The resurrection of Christ, as De Wette, the great German rationalist, himself admitted, can no more be brought into doubt by honest historic evidence than can the assassination of Cæsar. The external and the internal evidence of Christianity prove the divine authority of our Lord. His divine authority proves the doctrines he taught. Among these is immortality in the full sense of the word. It is the Scriptures which bring life and immortality into full light; but mere reason, in the present state of science, is able to show that there is no ground for believing that death ends all. — *Joseph Cook.*

March 10

We are quite sure
That He will give them back, — bright, pure
    and beautiful;
  We know He will but keep
  Our own and His until we fall asleep.
  We know He does not mean
  To break the strands reaching between
  The Here and There.
He does not mean, though Heaven be fair,
To change the spirits entering there, that they
    forget
  The eyes upraised and wet,
  The lips too still for prayer,
      The mute despair. . . .
      I do believe
      They will receive
  Us, — you and me, — and be so glad
To meet us, that when most I would grow sad
I just begin to think about that gladness,
      And the day
When they shall tell us all about the way
  That they have learned to go, —
      Heaven's pathways show.

George Klingle.

March 11

My lost, my own and I,
Shall have so much to see together by and by
I do believe that just the same sweet face,
But glorified, is waiting in the place
Where we shall meet, if only I
Am counted worthy in that by and by.
I do believe that God will give a sweet sur-
    prise
  To tear-stained, saddened eyes,
  And that his heaven will be
Most glad, most tided through with joy for
    you and me,
As we have suffered most.   God never made
Spirit for spirit, answering shade for shade,
  And placed them side by side, —
So wrought in one, though separate, mysti-
    fied, —
        And meant to break
The quivering threads between.   When we
    shall wake
I am quite sure we will be very glad
That for a little while we were so sad.

                    George Klingle.

March 12

The human soul is a substance, simple, indivisible, immaterial, spiritual, having subsistence and life in itself. This is proved by the nature of its highest operations. From the nature of an action we determine the essence of the agent. It follows, therefore, from the nature of human intelligence, that the human intellect is spiritual in its essence. As such, it is one of the indestructibles in nature, and the chief among all that exist on this earth. — *I. T. Hecker.*

However chilled in life's short, wintry day,
Through whose dull gloom the sun sends not
     its ray,
The heart of man is warm with joy divine
As night draws near, when stars of heaven
     shall shine.
          Adelaide Cilley Waldron.

March 13

Some time, when all life's lessons have been
    learned
And sun and stars for evermore have set,
The things which our weak judgments here
    have spurned —
The things o'er which we grieved with lashes
    wet —
Will flash before us, out of life's dark night,
As stars shine most in deeper tints of blue ;
And we shall see how all God's plans are
    right,
And how what seemed reproof was love most
    true.

And we shall shortly know that lengthened
    breath
Is not the sweetest gift God sends his friend,
And that sometimes the sable pall of death
Conceals the fairest boon his love can send.
If we could push ajar the gates of life
And stand within and all God's workings see,
We could interpret all this doubt and strife,
And for each mystery could find a key.

March 14

A final consideration, entitled to no little weight, is the need of faith in a life hereafter, to make this life tolerable. This hope is a necessity, whether one's thought centres on ourselves or our friends. Such a hope is not to be compared to the whimsical desires of men, born of their fashions or their appetites or their pride, but it takes hold of the deepest and holiest powers within us. If future life be not a reality, it follows that the most tremendous of untruths is essential to the present well-being of every human soul. Such a proposition is simply incredible.

A. A. Miner.

March 15

I watched a sail until it dropped from sight
   Over the rounding sea, — a gleam of light,
A last far-flashed farewell, and, like to thought
   Slipt.out of mind, it vanished and was not.

Yet, to the helmsman standing at the wheel,
   Broad seas still stretched before the gliding
       keel :
Disaster ? Change ? He left no slightest sign,
   Nor dreamed he of that dim horizon line.

So may it be, perchance, when down the tide
   Our dear ones vanish. Peacefully they glide
On level seas, nor mark the unknown bound.
   We call it death, — to them 't is life beyond.

March 16

But the supreme fact of all is the resurrection of the Saviour of mankind. He whose life was one of self-sacrifice; who endured scorn and persecution in silence; who laid down his life without a murmur, telling his followers that he would rise again, — all this, which, even now, shines so beautiful and clear, suddenly gives way if the resurrection be not a fact.

Accepted as a fact, no man need doubt the truth that "God is not a God of the dead, but of the living," nor fear to enter the Valley of the Shadow of Death under the guidance of Him who is "the Resurrection and the Life." — *Julian K. Smyth.*

March 17

Spirits escaped from the body can enter and
    be with the living;
Entering unseen and retiring unquestioned,
    they bring — do they feel, too ? —
Joy, pure joy, as they mingle and mix inner
    essence with essence.
Spirits with spirits commingle and separate;
    lightly as winds do,
Spice-laden south with the ocean-born zephyr,
    they mingle and sunder.

Clough.

And if but Faith and Hope are there,
    Why, what is death ?   To close our eyes,
To concentrate ourselves in prayer,
    To yield our souls to angels' care,
And sleep, to waken in the skies.

March 18

I consider the expectation of deathlessness an innate idea. Man has never been found without it. It is, therefore, an essential part of things that are. The future is as real as the present or the past. In fact there is no " future " nor " present " nor " past." These are but names of conditions. Man simply is alive and ever alive. " The hereafter " is a convenient name only. Such universal assent of all men, in all eras and places, makes " life hereafter " as certain as the universal assent of the present consciousness that we are, makes existence now a certainty. The Bible corroborates this essential idea, illustrates it, and teaches us the method of that life.

Emory J. Haynes.

Let not your heart be troubled. In my Father's house are many mansions. Because I live, ye shall live also.

It can hardly be gain for us to die, until it is Christ for us to live. — *Bascom.*

March 19

How shall we seem, each to the other, when,
  On that glad day, immortal we shall meet —
  Thou who long since didst pass with has-
      tening feet, —
I who still wait here, in the haunts of men?
Speech, — we shall need it not, nor language
      then ;
  Nor troth, which here conveyed its passion
      sweet ;
  Nor any signal from loved lips, to greet
In happy seal of loyalty.
                              Then, ken
Of the spirit, vision of the soul, will tell
  More than ecstatic pleadings in lost years ;
More than our trysting, with its magic spell ;
  Or faltering faith half perjured by pale
      fears :
From those all dross will then have fallen
      away,
And peerless love shall flood our souls that
      day.

Stephen Henry Thayer.

March 20

Man's moral sense is admitted to be the most exalted fact in his being; and the moral sense demands another world in which the wrongs of this are to be righted, — the arc to be made a circle. The Bible is true to us because it promises this. Man's reason demands the satisfaction of a conclusion of his life's logic; here we get but the two premises.

Man's affections demand the same. When conscience, reason, and love are content to end at the grave, man is no longer of sound mind.

Faith is but the assertion of these positions, "the substance of things hoped for." Faith is life. Despair is death. Faith is natural. Despair is unnatural, or disease or insanity.

Emory J. Haynes.

Our Lord has written the promise of the resurrection, not in books alone, but in every leaf in springtime. — *Martin Luther.*

March 21

Man being primarily a spiritual being, his own real progress or real success in life is as he so realizes himself. The life after death is fast coming to be no longer to us a speculation or a superstition, but a very real fact with which to deal — a phase of the near future for which to daily prepare. And the only true preparation for the life after death is to live nobly the life before death.

The evidence of immortality, and of sweet, swift communion between the visible and the invisible worlds, is in one's own soul.

Lilian Whiting.

We are led to the belief of a future state, not only by the weaknesses, by the hopes and fears of human nature, but by the noblest and best principles which belong to it, by the love of virtue and by the abhorrence of vice and injustice. — *Adam Smith.*

March 22

Life changes all our thoughts of heaven.
At first we think of streets of gold,
Of gates of pearl and dazzling light,
Of shining wings and robes of white,
And things all strange to mortal sight.
But in the afterward of years
It is a more familiar place,
A home unhurt by sighs or tears,
Where waiteth many a well-known face.
With passing months it comes more near,
It grows more real day by day,
Not strange or cold, but very dear, —
The glad home land not far away,
Where none are sick or poor or lone,
The place where we shall find our own.
And as we think of all we knew
Who there have met to part no more,
Our longing hearts desire home, too,
With all the strife and trouble o'er.

No work begun may ever pause with Death.
Browning.

The starry, moonless night looks on the
    heaving
    Of the sea, and hears its waters roll;
And I look out on both with troubled striving,
    To learn the aim and purpose of my soul.

I yearn towards the stars to catch their calm-
    ness,
    But the near sea still moaneth like my
    heart;
The distant skies, — are they too far above me
    Unto my soul their calmness to impart?

O give to me, ye stars! an earnest purpose, —
    To me give strength and energy of soul;
Make grand and bright my life with your still
    gleaming,
    That I forget the sea's long, troubled roll.

That I forget my heart's wild, useless yearn-
    ings,
    Its vain and vague repinings o'er lost hope,
Give to my mind its highest, best existence,
    Give to my soul its fullest aim and scope.

March 24

Enough that blessings undeserved
    Have marked my erring track,
That wheresoe'er my feet have swerved,
    His chastening turned me back;

That more and more a Providence
    Of love is understood,
Making the springs of time and sense
    Sweet with eternal good;

That death seems but a covered way
    Which opens into light,
Wherein no blinded child can stray
    Beyond the Father's sight.

Whittier.

When the commonplace " We must all die "
transforms itself suddenly into acute consciousness, " I must die " — and soon, — then
Death grapples us, and his fingers are cruel;
afterward he may come to fold us in his arms
as our mother did, and our last moment of
dim earthly discerning may be like the first.

George Eliot.

March 25

We turn with inexpressible relief, with perfect satisfaction, to Him who hath brought life and immortality to light. Rush-lights thrust into a grave do not dispel much of its gloom. In fact it is not the grave that needs the illumination, but the inmost soul of man. Man carries his light in his darkness within himself: the grave is just as bright as the fireside for the soul which is kindled within with the love of God, of Christ, of truth and purity and righteousness. " In thy light shall we see light; " " Because thou livest we shall live also." — *S. E. Herrick.*

Are not the stars like beacons set
   To guide the argosies that go
From universe to universe,
   Our little world above, below ? —
O thought too vast ! O thought too glad !
   An awe most rapturous stirs;
From world to world God's beacons shine :
   God means to save his mariners !

H. H.

March 26

Dear friend, far off, my lost desire,
   So far, so near in woe and weal;
   Oh, loved the most when most I feel
There is a lower and a higher;

Known and unknown, human, divine!
   Sweet human hand and lips and eye!
   Dear heavenly friend that canst not die,
Mine, mine, forever, ever mine;

Strange friend, past, present, and to be,
   Loved deeplier, darklier understood;
   Behold, I dream a dream of good,
And mingle all the world with thee.

Tennyson.

March 27

In this matter of the life to come, when I have thought and thought and sometimes become dazed with thinking, I turn to Christ: I see how his teachings are alive with this feeling of immortality; how he could never think of death except as a falling asleep, or as going to the Father. There I finally rest. Humanity at its highest, where it seems consciously to touch the divine, utters the same thought, which speaks in the dumb instincts of human nature at its lowest, — that this life is not all, that man is to live again.

Brooke Herford.

March 28

So sometimes comes to soul and sense
The feeling which is evidence,
That very near about us lies
The realm of spiritual mysteries.
The sphere of the supernal powers
Impinges on this world of ours.
The low and dark horizon lifts,
To light the scenic terror shifts;
The breath of a diviner air
Blows down the answer of a prayer,
That all our sorrow, pain, and doubt
A great compassion clasps about,
And law and goodness, love and force,
Are wedded fast beyond divorce.
Then duty leaves to love its task;
The beggar Self forgets to ask;
With smile of trust and folded hands,
The passive soul in waiting stands,
To feel, as flowers the sun and dew,
The one true Life its own renew.

Whittier.

March 29

Will my tiny spark of being wholly vanish in
    your deeps and heights?
Must my day be dark by reason, O ye
    heavens, of your boundless nights,
Rush of Suns, and roll of systems, and your
    fiery clash of meteorites?

Spirit nearing yon dark portal at the limit of
    thy human state,
Fear not thou the hidden purpose of that
    Power which alone is great;
Nor the myriad world, His shadow, nor the
    silent Opener of the Gate.
Tennyson.

Dark lattice! letting in eternal day.
Edward Young.

March 30

It would seem that the highest and holiest soul carries with it, like an atmosphere, a perfect serenity, a sense of present eternity, a presage of immortality. That sense is the perpetual sunlight which crowns the higher moral summits. We find the higher souls, and our own souls in their higher experiences, never stopping to question about it. Our doubts of unending life grow out of our earthiness. — *S. E. Herrick.*

Good, to be one of the angel choir,
    With never a shadow of shame or sin;
No bitter remembrance of earthly guilt
    To mar the untroubled peace within.
Better, to be a human soul,
    Won by the love of Christ to heaven;
Casting the crown, and striking the harp,
    And singing the song of the much-forgiven.
                        Gail Hamilton.

March 31

Again down life's dim labyrinth
   I grope my way alone,
While madly, through the midnight sky,
   Black, hurrying clouds are blown,
And thickly, in my tangled path,
   The sharp, bare thorns are sown.

Yet firm my foot, for well I know
   The goal cannot be far,
And ever, through the rifted clouds,
   Shines out one steady star;
For when my guide went up, he left
   The pearly gates ajar.

                Fanny Forrester.

April 1

Is it, then, regret for buried time
    That keenlier in sweet April wakes,
    And meets the year, and gives and takes
The colors of the crescent prime?

·Not all: the songs, the stirring air,
    The life re-orient out of dust,
    Cry thro' the sense to hearten trust
In that which made the world so fair.

Not all regret: the face will shine
    Upon me, while I muse alone;
    And that dear voice I once have known
Still speak to me of me and mine.

Yet less of sorrow lives with me
    For days of happy commune dead,
    Less yearning for the friendship fled,
Than some strong bond which is to be.

"Look at us," said the violets blooming at her feet. "All last winter we slept in seeming death, as your mother is sleeping now; but at the right time God awakened us, and here we are to comfort you." — *E. P. Roe.*

April 2

And while in life's late afternoon,
Where cool and long the shadows grow,
I walk to meet the night that soon
Shall shape and shadow overflow,
I cannot feel that thou art far,
Since near at need the angels are :
And when the sunset gates unbar
Shall I not see thee waiting stand,
And, white against the evening star,
The welcome of thy beckoning hand?
Whittier.

When the sun is setting, cool fall its gleams
upon the earth, and the shadows lengthen ;
but they all point toward the morning.
Jean Paul Richter.

April 3

Having looked at man and his earth, what remains to complete the greatness of the scene? Only one thing,—that there shall lie under him, in all these years, the power of an endless life. He does not want, nor seem to need, a life which may soon dissolve. He needs the power of an indissoluble existence. Society needs the moral conception and inspiration found in the belief in immortality. Our law, our right, our charity, our friendship, our religion, our inexpressible attachment, last for ages, not for days.

You are all justified in believing that a vision so grand and so beautiful will come true; you are all justified in believing that such a globe, full of seasons and covered with sunbeams, full of love and thought, is not simply a place in which a Christ may die, but a place from which his soul arises; you are justified in asking all the flowers of all the fields, and the spring sunbeams that make them, to assure you that under you, and all whom you love, flows the power of an endless life. — *David Swing.*

April 4

Our destiny, our being's heart and home,
Is with infinitude and only there;
With hope it is, hope that can never die,
Effort, and expectation, and desire,
And something evermore about to be.

Wordsworth.

The man who has constantly contended against evil, morally and physically, outwardly and inwardly, may fearlessly meet death; well assured that radiant spirits will lead him across the luminous bridge into a paradise of eternal happiness. . . . Souls risen from the graves will know each other, and say, That is my father, or my brother, my wife, or my sister. The wicked will say to the good, Wherefore, when I was in the world, did you not teach me to act righteously?   O ye pure ones, it is because you did not instruct me, that I am excluded from the assembly of the blest.

Zendavesta, Persian; Zoroaster. 589 B. C.

April 5

O may I join the choir invisible
Of those immortal dead who live again
In minds made better by their presence: live
In pulses stirred to generosity,
In deeds of daring rectitude, in scorn
For miserable aims that end with self,
In thoughts sublime that pierce the night like
     stars,
And with their mild persistence urge man's
     search
To vaster issues. — So to live is heaven:
To make undying music in the world,
Breathing as beauteous order, that controls
With growing sway the growing life of man.
     . . . This is life to come,
Which martyred men have made more glorious
For us who strive to follow.   May I reach
That purest heaven; be to other souls
The cup of strength in some great agony;
Enkindle generous ardor; feed pure love; . . .
Be the sweet presence of a good diffused,
And in diffusion ever more intense.
So shall I join the choir invisible,
Whose music is the gladness of the world.
George Eliot.

April 6

As kindred, friends, and dear ones salute him who hath traveled far and returned home safe, so will good deeds welcome him who goes from this world and enters another.

Dhammapada; Buddha Sakya; Hindu.
Born 627 B. C.

When thou shalt have laid aside thy body, thou shalt rise, freed from mortality, and become a god of the kindly skies.

Pythagoras; Grecian. Born 580 B. C.

My body must descend to the place ordained, but my soul will not descend: being a thing immortal, it will ascend on high, where it will enter a heavenly abode.

Heraclitus; Ephesian. 500 B. C.

April 7

O beautiful world! O good God! Such a day is the promise of a blissful eternity. Our Creator never would have made such weather, and have given us the deep heart to enjoy it, above and beyond all thought, if he had not meant us to be immortal. It opens the gates of heaven and gives us glimpses far inward. — *Hawthorne*, 1843.

Each coming spring, forcing the sprouts of plants out of the earth, gives me explanation of the awful riddle of death, and contradicts my anxious fears about an everlasting sleep. The swallow that we find stiffened in winter, and see waking up to life after; the dead grub coming to life again as the butterfly and rising into the air, — all these give excellent pictures of our immortality.

Schiller.

April 8

Good to forgive,
  Best to forget!
Living we fret,
  Dying we live.
Fretless and free,
  Soul, clap thy pinion!
Earth have dominion,
  Body, o'er thee.

Wander at will,
  Day after day —
Wander away,
  Wandering still —
Soul that canst soar!
  Body may slumber:
Body shall cumber
  Soul flight no more.

Waft of soul's wing!
  What lies above?
Sunshine and love,
  Sky-blue and spring!
Body hides — where?
  Ferns of all feather,
Mosses and heather,
  Yours be the care!

April 9

Eternal youth, beauty, strength, think of it, — free from the hampering, hindering body, living, learning, growing, and rejoicing!

M. W. B.

There are treasures laid up in the heart, — treasures of charity, piety, temperance, and soberness. These treasures a man takes with him beyond death, when he leaves this world.

Buddhist Scriptures; Ceylon.

Man never dies. The soul inhabits the body for a time, and leaves it again. The soul is myself; the body is only my dwelling-place. Birth is not birth; there is a soul already existent when the body comes to it. Death is not death; the soul merely departs, and the body falls. It is because men see only their bodies that they love life and hate death. — *Buddhist Scriptures; Chinese.*

April 10

Within the beggar's bare and bleak abode,
    As freely as in homes of guarded ease;
    On ships that labor over billowy seas,
As to the town's turmoil, or quiet road
Through sheltered villages of ancient mode;
    On mountain heights and in fair furrowed
        leas;
    To him who thee forgets, or sad foresees
Thy sure approach, O Death, — thy feet have
        strode,
Unheeding bruisèd blossoms in thy way,
    Whene'er the singled soul has heard its call
From Him whose hand alone thy touch can
        stay :
    To his omnipotence thou too thy thrall
Must only yield, and, lo ! thy sceptre's sway
    But points to heaven that shineth for us all!
                A. C. Waldron.

We are happy, for we belong to eternity.
                Von Auerbach.

April 11

There are so many souls! What world can hold them all? What care can recognize, and cover, and embrace them all? The thought of one's own immortality sinks like a tired soldier on a battle-field, overwhelmed and buried under the multitude of the dead. Have not many of you felt this bewilderment? What can we say to it? How can we grasp and believe in this countless army of immortals who come swarming up out of all the lands and all the ages? There is only one way. Multiply numbers as enormously as you will, and the result is finite still. Then set the finite, however large, into the presence of the infinite, and it is small. Its limitations show. There is no finite, however vast, that can overcrowd the infinite; none that the infinite cannot most easily grasp and hold. Here must be the real solution of our difficulty, in the infinity of God.

Phillips Brooks.

April 12

O glorious day when I shall remove from this confused crowd to join the divine assembly of souls! For I shall go not only to meet great men, but also my own son Cato. His spirit, looking back upon me, departed to that place whither he knew that I should soon come; and he has never deserted me. If I have borne his loss with courage, it is because I consoled myself with the thought that our separation would not be for long.

Cato (as quoted by Cicero); Roman. Born 243 B. C.

Although the eternal spirit dwells in the cell of every tree or flower, and in every human heart, it is undivided, and in its unity fills the world. He whose thoughts dwell in the infinite, regards the world as the mighty corolla from which the thought of God exhales. — *Von Auerbach.*

April 13

Naked from out that far abyss behind us
    We entered here:
No word came with our coming, to remind us
    What wondrous world was near,
      No hope, no fear.

Into the starless, silent Night before us
    Naked we glide;
No hand has mapped the constellations o'er us,
    No comrade at our side,
      No chart, no guide.

Yet fearless toward that midnight black and
      hollow
    Our footsteps fare:
The beckoning of a Father's hand we follow,
    His love alone is there,
      No curse, no care.

Edward R. Sill.

April 14

There is within us an immaterial being, an exile in our bodies, which it is destined to survive eternally. This being of purer essence and a better nature is our soul. It is this which gives birth to all enthusiasms, all affections, which apprehends God and heaven.

Victor Hugo.

To me, death is no longer dreadful; for me it has lost all its terrors; it is only a brief pain of separation from our beloved. It has grown to be no more to me than when my friend crosses the ocean to the other hemisphere. I miss him dreadfully, the days seem long till the sweet time when I shall again see him; but I know he is there, and never forgets me any more than I forget him, and that presently I shall join him;—the longest time is brief; and it is said, in that beautiful new life our darlings have begun, there is no time; the word means nothing to them any longer.

Celia Thaxter.

April 15

Believing, in the midst of our afflictions,
That death is a beginning, not an end,
We cry to them, and send
Farewells that better might be called predic-
        tions,
Being foreshadowings of the future, thrown
Into the vast Unknown.

Faith overleaps the confines of our reason,
And if by faith, as in old times was said,
Women received their dead
Raised up to life, then only for a season
Our partings are, nor shall we wait in vain
Until we meet again.

                        Longfellow.

April 16

This earthly life, when seen hereafter from heaven, will seem like an hour passed long ago and dimly remembered; long, laborious, full of joys and sorrows as it is, it will then have dwindled down to a mere point, hardly visible to the far-reaching ken of the disembodied spirit. And thus death is neither an end nor a beginning. It is a transition, not from one existence to another, but from one state of existence to another.

O that thou didst look forward to the great hereafter with half the longing wherewith thou longest for an earthly future, which a few days, at most, will bring thee, to the meeting of the dead as to the meeting of the absent! Thou glorious spirit-land! O that I could behold thee as thou art, — the region of life and light and love and the dwelling-place of those beloved ones whose being has flowed onward like a silver-clear stream into the solemn-sounding main, into the ocean of Eternity! — *Anne C. L. Botta.*

April 17

"How shall we bury you?" said a friend to Socrates. "Just as you please," said he with a smile, "if only you can catch me and I do not escape you." Here, as always, his pleasantry was the cool expression of his strongest faith. Not a particle of his frame has perished in the great treasury of matter. And has that mind dissolved, that robust spiritual greatness, that muscular, invincible holiness, that inward eye which saw the light of eternal truth as the steady flame of a zenith star? ... And is the Almighty so penurious of matter, and so wasteful of the wealth of perfect virtue, that he saves carefully each ounce of saintly servants' bodies, and permits their souls to be extinguished forever by a gill of poison, or shriveled by a fever, or consumed in a wreath of flame? We had better not believe that until we have emptied the universe of all that is divine. The life, the moral greatness, of Socrates is an argument for immortality such as logic could not frame, nor skepticism destroy; and thus his prison is a bright spot in human history, for it is a buttress of the soul's immortal hope. — *Starr King.*

April 18

Depart, drear visions of the night!
We are the dead, not they.
High in God's mansions of delight
They greet immortal day.
Look out!   The sky is flushed with gold,
In glad celestial warning!
The cloudy bars are backward rolled,
And, gloom and shadows scorning,
Above all glories glorious,
Comes up the Easter morning.

This life! — what is it but a single bloom
In the wide summer's wilderness of flowers?
The faintest star of all that light the gloom, —
One shuttle-cast of God's untiring loom, —
One flying moment in immortal hours?
And death, that we bewail as bitter doom,
What but the gift of unimagined dowers?
God were not God else.   Let us welcome,
        then,
The smiting angel, and our fears assuage;
How sharp soe'er his summons, cry "Amen,"
And go to gain the nobler heritage.

Edna Dean Proctor.

April 19

Music is the universal language of the innermost spiritual nature. All that we cultivate of its highest spirit in its great religious expressions here will go with us as preparation for eternity. We shall slough off, probably, our English vocabulary and tongue in the grave; but, even in the final gathering of the redeemed out of every nation, tongue, and clime, one strophe of the consummate Anthem to the Lamb, and through him to the Infinite, may be the Hallelujah Chorus of the Messiah, contributed from this earth to form part of the everlasting language of the skies.— *Starr King.*

The voices of the day
Are heard across the voices of the dark;
No sudden heaven nor sudden hell for man,
But through the will of one who knows and
     rules —
And utter knowledge is but utter love —
Æonian evolution, swift or slow
Through all the spheres, — an ever-opening
     height,
An ever-lessening earth.
               Tennyson.

April · 20

The stars steal, slow and silent,
Each in the ancient place,
Each in armor shining,
The hosts of heaven arrayed,
And wheeling through the midnight
As they did when the world was made.

And I lean out among the shadows
Cast by that far white gleam,
And I tremble at the murmur
Of one mote in the mighty beam,
As the everlasting squadrons
Their fated influence shed,
While the vast meridians sparkle
With the glory of their tread.
That constellated glory
The primal morning saw,
And I know God moves to his purpose,
And still there is life in his law.

Harriet Prescott Spofford.

April 21

When I forth fare beyond this narrow earth,
  With all its metes and bounds of now and
      here,
  And brooding clouds of ignorance and fear
That overhung me on my day of birth,
Wherethrough the jocund sun's perennial
      mirth
  Has shone more inly bright each coming
      year
  With some new glory of that outer sphere
Where length and breadth and height are little
      worth,
Then shall I find that even here below
  We guessed the secret of eternity,
  And learned in years the yearless mystery;
For in our earliest world we came to know
  The master-lesson and the riddle's key:
  Unending love unending growth shall be.
                    Charles F. Richardson.

April 22

You do like to do good, and live a life worth living, and when you get to heaven you will always want to do exactly the thing by which you can best please the dear Lord. The fashions there in heaven are set by Him who made himself of no reputation, and came and spent years among poor, ignorant, stupid, wicked people, that He might bring them up to himself: and I dare say the saints are burning with zeal to be sent on such messages to our world; I don't think they "sit on every heavenly hill," paying compliments to each other, but they are flying hither and thither on messages of mercy to the dark, the desolate, the sorrowful. That's the way you'll be when you get there, and, spite of all you say about yourself, you'll get to liking that sort of work more and more here.

H. B. Stowe.

April 23

The planted seed, consigned to common earth,
Disdains to moulder with the baser clay,
But rises up to meet the light of day;
Spreads all its leaves, and flowers, and tendrils
    forth,
And, bathed and ripened in the genial ray,
Pours out its perfume on the wand'ring gales,
Till in that fragrant breath its life exhales.
So this immortal germ within my breast
Would strive to pierce the dull, dark clod of
    sense
With aspirations wingèd and intense;
Would so stretch upwards in its tireless quest
To meet the central Soul, its source, its rest:
So in the fragrance of the immortal flower,
High thoughts and noble deeds, its life it would
    outpour.

Anne C. L. Botta.

April 24

Is it a misfortune to pass from infancy to youth? Still less can it be a misfortune to go from this miserable life to that true life into which we are introduced by death. Our first changes are connected with the progressive development of life. The new change which death effects is only the passage to a more desirable perfection. To complain of the necessity of dying is to accuse Nature of not having condemned us to perpetual infancy.

Gregory of Nyssa; Early Christian Father. 394 A. C.

Some people think of childhood as immeasurably beneath and behind them. I have never been able to join in such a notion. It often seems to me that we lose quite as much as we gain by our lengthened sojourn here. I should not at all wonder if the thoughts of our childhood, when we look back on it after the rending of this veil of our humanity, should prove less unlike what we were intended to derive from the teaching of life, nature, and revelation than the thoughts of our more sophisticated days. — *Jean Ingelow.*

April 25

“Let the bloom
Of Life grow over, undenied,
This bridge of Death, which is not wide,—
I shall be soon at the other side.

“Glory to God—to God!” he saith—
“Knowledge by suffering entereth,
And life is perfected by Death!”

Mrs. Browning.

So shall I lift up in my piercèd hands,
Not into dark, but light,—not unto death,
But life,—beyond the reach of guilt and
  grief,
The whole creation.

Mrs. Browning.

April 26

Can the soul be destroyed? No. But if in this present life it has shunned being governed by the body, and has governed itself within itself, and has separated from the body in a pure state, taking nothing sensual away with it, does it not then depart to that which resembles itself, — to the invisible, the divine, the wise, the immortal? And on its arrival there, is it not freed from errors, ignorance, fears, wild passions, and all other human evils? Does it not in truth pass the rest of its existence with the gods? . . .

Those who have lived a holy life, when they are freed from this earth, and set at large, as it were from a prison, will arrive at a pure abode above, and live without bodies through all future time. They will arrive at habitations more beautiful than it is easy to describe. — *Plato; Grecian.* 429 B. C.

April 27

Like the rise and set of the starry host,
Earth's myriads come and go;
Yet whence we speed through the infinite
        spaces, —
Speed as the light, and leave no traces, —
And what the calm on the pale, cold faces,
And whither we pass to our shining places
By far celestial isle and coast,
O Lord, we may not know.

But we are thine, and thy peace descends
As our hearts cry out to thee;
Peace, sigh the winds o'er the lone graves
        blowing;
And we know that the stars, the azure strew-
        ing,
And the souls whose life is thy bestowing,
Forever and ever to thee are going,
To the Love that rise and set attends,
And the Glory that is to be.

                    Edna Dean Proctor.

April 28

We go to the grave of a friend saying, "A man is dead," but angels throng about him saying, "A man is born." — *H. W. Beecher.*

We sometimes congratulate ourselves at the moment of waking from a troubled dream: it may be so after death. — *Hawthorne.*

What if earth
Be but the shadow of heaven? and things therein
Each to the other like, more than on earth is thought?

John Milton.

It is only just passing from one country to another. . . . There is not so much difference, I fancy, between this life and the next, as we think, nor so much barrier. I shall look in upon you in the new rooms some day; but you will not see me. — *Helen Hunt.*

April 29

Of what import this vacant sky, these puffing elements, these insignificant lives, full of selfish loves, and quarrels, and ennui? Everything is prospective, and man is to live hereafter. That the world is for his education is the only sane solution of the enigma. All the comfort I have found teaches me to confide that I shall not have less in times and places that I do not yet know. I have known admirable persons, without feeling that they exhaust the possibilities of virtue and talent. I have seen glories of climate, of summer mornings and evenings, of midnight sky; I have enjoyed the benefits of all this complex machinery of arts and civilization, and its results of comfort. The Good Power can easily provide me millions more as good. All I have seen teaches me to trust the Creator for all I have not seen. Whatever it be which the great Providence prepares for us, it must be something large and generous, and in the great style of his works.

R. W. Emerson.

April 30

With sails full set, the ship her anchor weighs.
Strange names shine out beneath her figure-
 head.
What glad farewells with eager eyes are said!
What cheer for him who goes, and him who
 stays !
Fair skies, rich lands, new homes, and un-
 tried days
Some go to seek; the rest but wait instead
Until the next stanch ship her flag doth raise.
Who knows what myriad colonies there are
Of fairest fields, and rich, undreamed-of gains,
Thick planted in the distant shining plains
Which we call sky because they lie so far?
Oh, write of me, not " Died in bitter pains,"
But " Emigrated to another star."

Helen Hunt.

May 1

Why, Death, what dost thou here
  This time o' the year? . . .

Dark Death let fall a tear:
  "Why am I here?
O heart ungrateful, will man never know
I am his friend and never was his foe?
Whose the sweet season, then, if it be not
      mine?
Mine, not the bobolink's, that voice divine
Chasing the shadows o'er the bending wheat:
'T is a dead voice, not his, that sings so sweet.
Whose wanhope pales that nun-like Lily tall,
  Beside the garden wall,
But hers, whose radiant eyes and slender grace
Sleep in the grave that crowns yon tufted hill?
    All hope, all memory,
    Have their deep springs in me,
    And love, that else might fade,
    By me immortal made,
Spurns at the grave, leaps to the welcoming
      skies,
And burns a steadfast star to steadfast eyes.
                              Clarence Cook.

May 2

He who is preparing us for our heaven is preparing our heaven for us. What a beautiful world this is in which we live this May day, so full of sunshine and song! But think! This is the prison; what will the palace be? This is the ocean steamer; what will the home be? This is the wilderness; what will the land of promise be? If this is what God made for the schoolroom, I wonder what he has made for the home. Sometimes I wish I knew, but on the whole I am glad I do not. I am glad that, when awaking comes, I shall awake to a glad surprise. — *Lyman Abbott.*

Love, Rest, and Home!
Lord, tarry not, but come!

May 3

I cannot believe in heaven and not believe in the recognition of friends there; for there would be no heaven if there were no recognition of friends. What does Paul mean when he says, " Faith and hope and love abide forever " ? Love of the father, love of the mother, love of the wife, love of the husband, love of the friend, with all the hungering desire of love and nothing to satisfy it ! That would be hell, not heaven. You remember that on the Mount of Transfiguration the disciples recognized Moses and Elijah. Do you suppose that Moses and Elijah did not know each other ?

Lyman Abbott.

Come let us join our friends above
  That have obtained the prize,
And on the eagle wings of love
  To joy celestial rise.

Charles Wesley.

May 4

I remember a remark you once made on spiritualism. I cannot recall the words, but you spoke of it as modifying the sharp angles of Calvinistic belief, as a fog does those of a landscape. I would like to talk with you on spiritualism, and show you a collection of very curious facts that I have acquired through mediums not professional. I have long since come to the conclusion that the marvels of spiritualism are natural and not supernatural phenomena, — an uncommon working of natural laws. I believe that the door between those *in* the body and those *out* has never in any age been entirely closed, and that occasional perceptions within the veil are a part of the course of nature, and therefore not miraculous.

Letter to Dr. Holmes from Mrs. Stowe.

May 5

They think me daft who nightly meet
My face turned starward, while my feet
Stumble along the unseen street;

But should man's thoughts have only room
For Earth, his cradle and his tomb,
Not for his Temple's grander gloom?

And must the prisoner, all his days,
Learn but his dungeon's narrow ways,
And never through its grating gaze?

Then let me linger in your sight,
My only amaranths! blossoming bright
As over Eden's cloudless night;

The same vast belt, and square, and crown
That on the Deluge glittered down,
And lit the roofs of Bethlehem town.

E. R. Sill.

May 6

Beauty abides, nor suffers mortal change,
Eternal refuge of the orphaned mind:
Where'er, a lonely wanderer, I range,
The tender flowers shall my woes unbind,
   The grass to me be kind;
And lovely shapes innumerable shall throng
On sea and prairie, soft as children's eyes;
Morn shall awake me with her glad surprise;
   The stars shall hear my song;
And heaven shall I see whate'er my road,
Steadfast, eternal, light's impregnable abode.
G. E. Woodberry.

To leave behind and drop off all our present knowledge would not be immortality, but the death of our present character and the creation of another being. The law of life is development, not destruction; unfolding of what we are now into something higher, but not dropping off anything important, or leaving it behind. — *James Freeman Clarke.*

May 7

Love, too, abides, and smiles at savage Death,
And swifter speeds his might and shall endure
The secret flame, the unimagined breath,
That lives in all things beautiful and pure,
      Invincibly secure :
In Him creation hath its glorious birth,
Subsists, rejoices, moves prophetic on,
Till that dim goal of all things shall be won
Men yearn for through the earth;
Voices that pass we are of Him, the Song
Whose harmonies the winds, the stars, the
      seas prolong.
              G. E. Woodberry.

Death's cold white hand is like the snow
    Laid softly on the furrowed hill,
It hides the broken seams below
    And leaves the summit higher still.
              O. W. Holmes.

May 8

The Incarnation is one of God's consolations: that into the very midst of this broken order has entered in human form, with human sensibilities and human sympathies, the Lord Jesus Christ, to be tempted like as we are, to bear our griefs, to carry our sorrows, to taste death for every man, to show us in his Resurrection that there is victory in store for us; to lift up our eyes toward that new order, which is but the original order brought back across the chaos of sin and made once more the inheritance of redeemed humanity: "I am the Resurrection and the Life: he that believeth in me, though he were dead, yet shall he live, and whosoever liveth and believeth in me shall never die."

Charles Cuthbert Hall.

May 9

Dead? Not to thee, thou keen watcher, not
    silent, not viewless to thee.
Immortal still wrapped in the mortal, I, from
    the mortal set free,
Greet thee by many clear tokens thou smilest
    to hear and to see.

Once as a wall were the mountains, once
    darkened between us the sea;
No longer these thwart and baffle, forbidding
    my passage to thee:
Immortal still wrapped in the mortal, I linger
    till thou art set free.

Edith M. Thomas.

If, in a long life here, I have gained anything which is worth keeping, it is the knowledge and friendship and love of pure, generous,
noble souls. Am I to lose that great inheritance? Am I to go into the other world
poor, lonely, homesick, alone? I do not so
understand the lessons of experience, or the
facts of observation.

James Freeman Clarke.

May 10

Every idea we can form of Justice, Love, Duty, is truncated and imperfect if we deny them the extension of eternity; and as for our conception of God, I see not how any one who has realized " the riddle of the painful earth " can thenceforth call Him " good " unless he believe that the solution is yet to be given to that dark problem hereafter.

F. P. Cobbe.

I have got past the time when I feel that my heavenly friends are lost by going there. I feel them nearer, rather than farther off. If you see morning in our Father's house before I do, carry my love to those that wait for me; and if I pass first, you will find me there, and we shall love each other forever.

Mrs. Stowe.

All else of earth may perish; love alone
Not heaven shall find outgrown.

O. W. Holmes.

May 11

Edward Everett Hale was thus questioned by the Rev. H. M. Field: "How do you feel as you look forward to the future? Does it cast a shadow over you that life is coming to an end?" "Not in the least, for it is *not* coming to an end. We only pass from one stage to another. . . . I have not the slightest doubts as to a future life. On the contrary, I sometimes feel a longing to know what is beyond the veil, and am eager to see the curtain rise."

What shall death be to thee, O deathless soul?
　　Greatest it is of all the mysteries,
And yet it lieth in thine own control
　　To say how dark or else how bright it is.

Distance from God doth make the seeing dim.
　　Death need not be a plunge into the night,
But the short step that takes thee in to Him,
　　If thou live daily near the Lord of light.
　　　　　　　　　Charlotte Fiske Bates.

May 12

She had a divine discontent. Anybody can have a simply human discontent. Indeed, most people have, and little does it serve them. But she looked up so much into the great blue heavens that I think may be she was a little weaned from this world, for in the sky they tell us that there are two hundred million worlds. I think she was smitten in her soul with a thirst for immortality. And, really, there is nothing else worth living for, when one comes to think about it. If we are not immortal, if there is not a great free life beyond, as great as the outreaching of the heart, as great as the contriving of the brain, as great as the faith that fastens the aspiring soul to God, then we are the mightiest mockery that has been let loose to feed on its own anguish. — *Frances Willard.*

Again, how can she but immortal be,
When, with the motions of both will and wit,
She still aspireth to eternity,
And never rests till she attain to it ?
　　　　　Sir John Davies, 1570–1626.

May 13

"Eye hath not seen, ear hath not heard, it hath not entered into the imagination of the heart of man to conceive." Will you undertake to tell a little child studying the primer what is the glory of scholarship? Will you undertake to tell an Indian paddling his canoe what is the significance of an ocean steamer? Will you undertake to tell the bulb in the ground what is the beauty of the tulip when it has blossomed? Better try that than try to tell the men that are grubs in the chrysalis what the glorious flight in the sunshine will be. If this world is the chrysalis, what shall the sunshine and the flight become? I only know this: it will be so glorious in all outward beauty that the glorious things of this life will seem insignificant in comparison.

Lyman Abbott.

May 14

Yes, hope may with my strong desire keep
      pace,
And I be undeluded, unbetrayed;
For if of our affections none finds grace
In sight of Heaven, then wherefore hath God
      made
The world which we inhabit?   Better plea
Love cannot have than that in loving thee
Glory to that Eternal Peace is paid
Who such divinity to thee imparts
As hallows and makes pure all gentle hearts.
His hope is treacherous only whose love dies
With beauty, which is varying every hour;
But in chaste hearts, uninfluenced by the
      power
Of outward change, there blooms a deathless
      flower
That breathes on earth the air of Paradise.
   Michael Angelo, translated by Wordsworth.

May 15

Consider for a moment the foundation of our faith. "Ye have faith in God, have faith in me also." Christ does not talk of immortality as Socrates talked,—groping and hoping; he does not talk as the philosophers of to-day talk,—giving arguments pro and con, weighing, considering, and balancing them. He speaks as a witness: "In my Father's house are many mansions. In my Father's universe are many dwelling places." — I speak whereof I *know.* — *Lyman Abbott.*

Ye stars are but the shining dust
    Of my divine abode,
The pavements of those heavenly courts
    Where I shall reign with God.
                Philip Doddridge.

The evening brings all home. You and I, beloved, have just a little longer.

May 16

Who thoroughly understands anything which he cultivates, even to the flowers at his feet? And, cultivating these, shall we refuse to cultivate also the stars, and aspirations and thoughts angelical, and hopes of rejoining friends and kindred, and all the flowers of heaven? No, assuredly, — not while we have a star to see and a thought to reach it.

With regard to the belief in spirits, it has surely a right, even upon the severest grounds of reason, to rest upon the same privileges of possibility. . . . Had we possessed but two or three senses, we know very well that there are thousands of things round about us of which we could have formed no conception; and does not common modesty, as well as the possibilities of infinitude, demand of us that we should suppose there are senses besides our own, and that, with the help of but one more, we might become aware of phenomena at present unmanifested to human eyes? — *Leigh Hunt.*

May 17

No mortal object did these eyes behold
When first they met the placid light of thine,
And my soul felt her destiny divine,
And hope of endless peace in me grew bold :
Heaven-born, the soul a heavenward course
       must hold.
Beyond the visible world she soars to seek
(For what delights the sense is false and weak)
Ideal Form, the universal mould.
The wise man, I affirm, can find no rest
In that which perishes ; nor will he lend
His heart to aught that doth on time depend.
'T is sense, unbridled will, and not true love,
That kills the soul : love betters what is best,
Even here below, but more in heaven above.
  Michael Angelo, translated by Wordsworth.

May 18

You have been down by this great lake of ours and seen how the ship goes out and out, and sinks and sinks, and after a while the white sail is seen no more, and you say to yourself, " It is gone ! " But no, it is not gone. That good ship had a captain, and there was a hand upon the helm. They did not notice that vanishing, artificial horizon ; that was simply the place where your sight failed. So let us comfort one another with these words, and be glad of immortality, and of all those who have loved it, as all great souls have done.

Frances Willard.

Our passions, our endeavors, have something ridiculous and mocking if we come to so hasty an end. If not to be, how like the bells of a fool is the trump of fame! Will you, with vast cost and pains, educate your children to be adepts in their special arts, and, as soon as they are ready to produce a masterpiece, call out a file of soldiers to shoot them down ? — *Black.*

May 19

When the soul dumb with sorrow and darkened with the tears of grief cries out: "Wilt thou show wonders to the dead? Shall the dead arise and praise thee? Shall thy loving kindness be declared in the grave, or thy faithfulness in destruction? Shall thy wonders be known in the dark? and thy righteousness in the land of forgetfulness?" the Christ answers: "There are no dead — there are only living; there is no land of destruction — only a land of emancipation; there is no dark — only the land of greater light; there is no forgetfulness — only the land of sweet, sacred memories."

Lyman Abbott.

Look to thy soul, O man, for none can be
    surety for his brother;
Behold, — for heaven or for hell, — thou canst
    not escape from Immortality

Tupper.

May 20

"Till death us part." . . .

Till death us join!
O word yet more divine,
Which to the breaking heart breathes hope
    sublime!
Through wasted hours,
And shattered powers,
We still are one, despite of change and time.

Death with his healing hand
Shall knit once more the band,
Which needs but that one link that none may
    sever;
Till through the only Good
Seen, felt, and understood,
The life in God shall make us one forever.

Dean Stanley.

May 21

Death reads the title clear
What each soul for itself conquered from out
    things here.

As age, youth,
So death completes living, shows life in its
    truth.

                        Soul,
Nothing has been that shall not bettered be
Hereafter.

And I shall behold thee face to face,
O God, and in thy light re-trace
How in all I loved here still wast Thou!
                      Browning.

May 22

In the simplest way, Mrs. Stowe affirmed her entire belief in possible manifestations of the nearness and individual life of those who had passed to the unseen world, and gave vivid illustrations of the reason why her faith was thus assured. At that period, such a declaration of faith required a good deal of bravery; now the subject has assumed a different phase, and there are few thinking persons who do not recognize a certain truth hidden within the shadows. She spoke with tender seriousness of such manifestations as are recorded in the Old and New Testament. — *Annie Fields.*

In some hour of solemn jubilee
The massy gates of Paradise are thrown
Wide open, and forth come, in fragments wild,
Sweet echoes of unearthly melodies. . . .
And they that from the crystal river of life
Sprung up on freshened wing, ambrosial gales.
The favored good man in his lonely walk
Perceives them, and his silent spirit drinks
Strange bliss, which he shall recognize in
heaven.

Coleridge.

May 23

You never know what life means till you die;
Even throughout life, 't is death that makes
       life live,
Gives it whatever the significance —
Unmanned, remade, I hold it probable —
With something changeless at the heart of me
To know me by, some nucleus that 's myself.

            What were life,
Did soul stand still therein, forego her strife
Through the ambiguous Present to the goal
Of some all-reconciling Future?

Browning.

May 24

We pass from glory to glory, and that crisis which we call death is only a transition from one harmony to another. In certain forms of the Polish national dances, the guests move from room to room in the palace, the music and the movement ever changing in the processional march, according to the progressive phases of the theme enacted. From beginning to end it is the same theme, and the guests are the same. So may it be in the progression of our human life from one mansion to another of the Father's house; there is a mystic change, not of personalities, but of special individual guises, involving complete divestiture, the theme enacted remaining the same. — *H. M. Alden.*

May 25

It must be very near, that other land
   Upon whose very edge we stand,
   And they pass in at some command
We hear not, but their quick ears understand.

It must be very fair, that other shore,
   To win from what they held so dear,
   From us, who fain would hold them here,
Our best; to leave us and come back no
      more.

It must be very full, that other world,
   Into whose calm and sheltered ports
   Ships rich with freight of various sorts
Sail in from stormy seas with sails all furled.

May 26

Ye make it nearer, O beloved friends,
    Whose very dearness draws our hearts.
    To build, across the gulf that parts,
Some bridge to pass to where the parting ends.

Ye make it fairer, as your presence here
    Made this world fair; so Paradise
    Gains added beauty to our eyes
That strain to see you, blind with many a tear.

Ye make it fuller; God hath willed it so.
    Ye are our treasures storèd there;
    And He himself hath said it, — where
The treasure is, the heart will surely go.

Nearer and fuller and more fair to me,
    Dear land, calm shore, fair world, thou art :
    Let thy sweet charm draw us apart
From earth, and time, and sin, to dwell in
      thee.

May 27

Not thee we mourn, O friend, as fall the
tears;
Thine is the rest, the glory, and the gain:
We grieve that we, more lonely, walk the
years
And weaker turn to earthly toil and pain.

But brighter are the skies since thou art there,
Warmer the welcome after parting tears;
The farewell that we breathe uplifts the
prayer
That soon may dawn for us God's golden
years.

Wm. R. Duryee.

When bursts the rose of the spirit
From its withering calyx sheath,
And the bud has become a blossom
Of heavenly color and breath,
Life utters its true revelation
Through the silence that we call death.

May 28

We are not to think of heaven as at an infinite remove. It is very near to us. The same laws of divine goodness prevail there as here. Heaven and earth are provinces of one blessed kingdom. The change is from the basement story, where the heat and noise and dust of labor perplex and weary, to the lofty chambers which command the glorious sunset views and look away to the sun-rising, and are open to healthful winds and the song of birds. We are ourselves, it may be, on the stairway; we have been far up where it seemed as though a slight shock would burst open the door and let us through. — *J. O. Means.*

Mr. Moody said in closing : " I don't expect to die. If the paper says that D. L. Moody is dead, don't believe it. I may move out of this house, but I have something better than death."

May 29

Whence come we ?   Whither do we go ?
  What fetters these that bind us round ?
Must wisdom's end be not to know,
  And life be quenched in graveyard ground ?

From heights above there comes the thrill,
  O breath of God ! from out that height :
Blow fresh and strong upon the chill
  And darkness of this earth-born night.

One rushing blast renews the soul,
  And fear and terror melt away ;
Faith sees beyond the grave its goal,
  Love soars in song upon the way.

Wm. R. Duryee.

May 30

I with uncovered head
Salute the sacred dead
Who went and who return not. — Say not so!
'T is not the grapes of Canaan that repay,
But the high faith that failed not by the way :
Virtue treads paths that end not in the grave ;
No bar of endless night exiles the brave.

. . . .

Blow, trumpets, all your exultations blow !
For never shall their aureoled presence lack :
I see them muster in a gleaming row,
With ever youthful brows that nobler show :
We find in our dull road their shining track ;
In every nobler mood
We feel the orient of their spirit glow,
Part of our life's unalterable good, —
Of all our saintlier aspiration :
They come transfigured back,
Secure from change in their high-hearted ways,
Beautiful evermore, and with the rays
Of morn on their white Shields of Expecta-
tion !

J. R. Lowell.

May 31

Not here, beset by many a fear,
　　Find I my lasting home;
So often tempted from the narrow way,
So often wandering from that path astray,
So oft despairing on some gloomy day
　　Lest sunlight never come.

More fair, within a purer air,
　　My lasting home I find;
Promised by Lips which never framed deceit,
Prepared by Power which never knew defeat,
Glowing with Love beyond all love complete,
　　Around my Lord combined!

O Night, pass quickly — for the light
　　Of day eternal gleams —
From His dear Face which human pain has
　　　　known,
But waiting now to welcome to His throne,
From saints who find the rest supreme, alone,
　　Surpassing all our dreams.
　　　　　　　　Wm. R. Duryee.

June 1

The birds are glad, the brier rose fills
The air with sweetness, all the hills
Stretch green to June's unclouded sky;
But still I wait with ear and eye
For something gone which should be nigh,
A loss in all familiar things,
In flower that blooms and bird that sings.
And yet, dear heart, remembering thee,
Am I not richer than of old?
Safe in thy immortality,
What change can reach the wealth I hold?
What change can mar the pearl and gold
Thy love hath left in trust for me?

Whittier.

Even for the dead I will not bind
    My soul to grief, death cannot long divide;
For is it not as if the rose that climbed
    My garden wall had bloomed the other side?

Anon.

June 2

In life our absent friend is far away,
But death may bring our friend exceeding near,
Show him familiar faces long so dear,
And lead him back in reach of words we say.
He only cannot utter yea or nay,
In any voice accustomed to our ear;
He only cannot make his face appear
And turn the sun back on our shadowed day.
The dead may be around us, — dear and dead,
The unforgotten dearest dead may be
Watching us with unslumbering eyes and heart,
Brimful of words which cannot yet be said,
Brimful of knowledge they may not impart,
Brimful of love for you and love for me.

Christina Rossetti.

No good thing is ever lost. Nothing dies, not even life, which gives up one form only to resume another. No good action, no good example, dies. It lives forever in our race. While the frame moulders and disappears, the deed leaves an indelible stamp, and moulds the very thought and will of future generations.

Samuel Smiles.

June 3

To him who believes in immortality, Death is a deep, mysterious change, — but not the end of life. See how free it makes him! He can undertake works of self-culture, or the development of truth far, far too vast for the earthly life of any Methuselah to finish, and yet smile calmly and work on when men tell him that he will die before his work is done. Die! Shall not the sculptor sleep a hundred times before the statue he begins to-day is finished, and wake a hundred times more ready for his work, bringing with a hundred new mornings to his work the strength and the visions that have come to him in his slumber?

Phillips Brooks.

The gift of God is eternal life through Jesus Christ our Lord. — *Romans, vi. 23.*

June 4

O silent stars! that over ages past
Have shone serenely as ye shine to-night,
Unseal, unseal the secret that ye keep!
Is it not time to tell us why we live?
Through all these shadowy corridors of years,
(Like some gray priest, who through the
       Mysteries
Led the blindfolded Neophyte in fear), —
Time leads us blindly onward, till in wrath
Tired Life would seize and throttle its stern
       guide,
And force him tell us *whither* and *how long*.
But Time gives back no answer — only points
With motionless finger to eternity,
Which deepens over us, as that deep sky
Darkens above me: only its vestibule
Glimmers with scattered stars; and down the
       west
A silent meteor slowly slides afar,
As though, pacing the garden walks of heaven,
Some musing seraph had let fall a flower.

                    E. R. Sill.

June 5

The stars move on along their giant path
Mysteriously up, across, and down,
And on their silver disks, meantime, God
      works
His holy wonders so mysteriously !
For, lo ! in blossom-laden twigs, the while,
The bird sleeps undisturbed; him wakeneth not
That mighty sweep of vast activity ;
No sound brings tidings of it down to earth;
No echo hear'st thou in the silent groves ! . . .
And thou, O man, desirest idle fame ?
Thou dost whate'er thou dost so noisily,
And childishly wouldst write it on the stars !
But let that gentle spirit enter thee,
Which from the sun's noiselessly mighty work,
From earth and spring, from moon and starry
      night,
Speaks to thy soul, — then thou too art at rest,
Doing thy good things and creating fair,
And going so still along thy earthly way,
As if thy soul were woven of moonlight,
Or thou wert one with that calm spirit above.

Ary Scheffer.

June 6

No shadows yonder,
   All light and song!
Each day I wonder,
   And say how long
Shall time me sunder
   From that dear throng?

No partings yonder,
   Time and space never
Again shall sunder;
   Hearts cannot sever,
Dearer and fonder
   Hands clasp forever.

Great love crosses even the shores of death. — *Propertius.*

June 7

I am looking for you.   Are you here?
　　All I see is sunshine, glad and clear,
Then a soft step seems to flit across the grass :
　　　　Did you pass?

Though I must remember your dear head
　　Lies below the grasses with the dead,
Yet, whene'er I pause to brush away a tear,
　　　　You seem here.

All the life I'm living is your own,
　　Sounds thro' midday stillness your sweet
　　　　tone,
And I seem to see in each familiar place
　　　　Your bright face.

.　　.　　.　　.　　.　　.　　.　　.

While the sunshine tells me you are near,
　　And the flowers whisper you are here,
Could I catch the music of the world where
　　you stay,
　　　　Were you far away?

June 8

In the presence of death I come back to the faithful and true witness, — to the one who was neither deceiver nor deceived, who spoke, not what he thought, but what he knew; and I believe in him and in his witness. As when one lies down upon an operating couch, and the surgeon about to administer the ether stoops over the patient and says, " Do not be troubled, do not be afraid; I have done this a thousand times; you will drop into unconsciousness for a few moments, then you will come back again, and you will not know what has happened to you, and you will suffer no twinge of pain," — so Christ stands by every bedside in the hour of the last releasing and says to his child, " Be not troubled, neither be afraid. I know you will drop into a moment of unconsciousness; you will wake from that unconsciousness into the new life, and you will know nothing of the quick transition." — *Lyman Abbott.*

June 9

The soul is immortal because it is fitted to rise towards that which is neither born nor dies, — towards that which exists substantially, necessarily, invariably ; that is to say, towards God. — *Amiel.*

Wait till that Angel comes who opens all,
The reconciler, he who lifts the veil,
The re-uniter, the rest-bringer, Death.
                    James Russell Lowell.

What if the days are dreary ?
    What if the desert glows
Beneath life's bitter sun-beat ?
    What if the wild wind blows
Out of the North-Land stormy ?
    What if Earth wears no smile ?
A gate will open outward
    In such a little while !
                    E. L. Beers.

June 10

We see all sights from pole to pole,
And glance and nod and hurry by,
And never once possess our soul
Until we die.
Matthew Arnold.

The conscious life, strong in its integrity, must go forth into the Unseen, bearing with it all love and wisdom gained on earth, trusting that, in the world of absolute knowledge, all desire shall be fulfilled, all doubt justified, and all truth revealed. — *Vida D. Scudder.*

Help me, O my God, continually to live as if I did not live, that so at last I may die as if I were not dying.

June 11

I shrink from the cold obstruction, — the oblivion of the grave. Like a timid child, I dread to go out alone into the darkness. The firelight on the hearthstone of home is more attractive to me than the brightest star in the far-off heavens. " The flight of a lone soul to a lone God" is a fearful thing to poor human nature. If, as the western " shadows fall longer" upon our earthly pathway, they were not met and dispersed by the auroral light of an immortal life, — a life made radiant and beautiful by the prospect of reunited human friendships, — then should we be of all men most miserable. — *Joseph G. Hoyt.*

Ye children, does Death e'er alarm you?
Death is the brother of Love, twin brother
Is he, and is only
More austere to behold.
      Henry Wadsworth Longfellow.

June 12

This is death.   I see the light no more,
I sleep.
       But like a morning bird my soul
Springs singing upward into the deeps of
    heaven,
Through world on world to follow Infinite
    Day.

Dinah Muloch Craik.

Through love to light!   Oh, wonderful the
    way
That leads from darkness to the perfect day,
From darkness and from sorrow of the night
To morning that comes singing o'er the sea.
Through love to light!—through light, O
    God, to thee,
Who art the love of love, the eternal light of
    light!

Richard Watson Gilder.

June 13

We are half heathen yet in our treatment of death. We surround it with gloom and blackness, and even while we repeat the words of faith, and commit our brother's body to the grave in sure and certain hope of immortality, we mourn as if from behind the veil had come forth the sentence, not Thy brother shall rise again, but The dead are dead forever; there is no hope for a man when he goeth down into the pit. It is time we learned better things than these. It is time that, amid inevitable tears and regrets of nature for our own loss and sorrow, we should see ever before us the rainbow on the cloud, and, knowing that our regrets are for ourselves alone, thank God, and take comfort in the faith that our lost ones beckon us from the abode where the eternal are. — *Frances Power Cobbe.*

June 14

I saw the stars swept through ethereal space,
Stars, suns, and systems in infinity, —
Our earth an atom in the shoreless sea,
Where each had its appointed path and place;
And I was lost in my own nothingness.
But then, I said, " Dost thou not know that
     He
Who guides these orbs through trackless space
     guides thee ? "

No longer groveling thús, thyself abase,
For in this vast, harmonious, perfect whole,
In infinite progression moving on,
Thou hast thy place, immortal human soul, —
Thy place and part not less than star and sun;
Then with this grand procession fall in line,
This rhythmic march led on by power divine.
                              Anne C. L. Botta.

June 15

Thou hast delivered her soul from anguish and death, her eyes from tears, and her feet from falling, and now she walks before Thee in the land of life. Dear was she to me, as Thou knowest, above all things in or of this world, the sun and joy of my house. And yet why should I weep for one from whose eyes all tears have been wiped away? Why mourn for her who shall mourn no more? I have lost a jewel in time, but I know it is kept in heaven; and I hope to recover it there, and to lose it no more forever.

Christian Scriver.

No! love which on earth amid all the shows
     of it,
Has ever been known the sole good of life in
     it,
That love, ever growing there spite of the
     strife in it,
Shall arise — made perfect — from Death's
     repose of it.

Robert Browning.

June 16

Ah, there is something here
Unfathomed by the cynic's sneer, —
Something that gives our feeble light
A high immunity from night,
Something that leaps life's narrow bars
To claim its birthright with the hosts of heaven.

.   .   .   .

A conscience more divine than we,
A gladness fed with secret tears,
A vexing, forward-reaching sense
Of some more noble permanence, —
A light across the sea,
Which haunts the soul and will not let it be,
Still glimmering from the heights of undegen-
     erate years.
                    James Russell Lowell.

He who, from zone to zone,
Guides through the boundless sky thy certain
     flight,
In the long way that I must tread alone,
     Will lead my steps aright.
                    William Cullen Bryant.

June 17

Since I am coming to that holy room,
Where with the choir of saints for evermore
I shall be made thy music, as I come
I tune the instrument at the door,
And what I must do then, think here before.

George Herbert.

Then long eternity shall greet our bliss
With an individual kiss,
And joy shall overtake us as a flood;
When everything that is sincerely good,
And perfectly divine,
With truth and peace and love shall ever
    shine
About the supreme throne
Of Him to whose happy-making sight alone,
When once our heavenly-guided soul shall
    climb,
Then, all this earthy grossness quit,
Attired with stars, we shall forever sit,
Triumphing over Death and Chance and thee,
    O Time!

John Milton.

June 18

With his illegitimate hypothesis of annihilation, the materialist transgresses the bounds of experience quite as widely as the poet who sings of the New Jerusalem with its river of life and its streets of gold. Scientifically speaking, there is not a particle of evidence for either view.

Are we to regard the Creator's work like that of a child, who builds houses out of blocks, just for the pleasure of knocking them down? I can see no good reason for believing any such thing. On such a view, the riddle of the universe becomes a riddle without a meaning. For my own part, therefore, I believe in the immortality of the soul, not in the sense in which I accept the demonstrable truths of science, but as a supreme act of faith in the reasonableness of God's work.

I feel the omnipresence of mystery in such wise as to make it far easier for me to adopt the view of Euripides, that what we call death may be but the dawning of true knowledge and of true life. — *John Fiske.*

June 19

Forever with the Lord.
    Amen! so let it be:
Life from the dead is in that word, —
    'T is immortality.
                James Montgomery.

Upon the frontier of this shadowy land
We pilgrims of eternal sorrow stand;
What realm lies forward, with its happier store
    Of forests green and deep,
    Of valleys hushed in sleep,
And lakes most peaceful? 'T is the land of
    evermore.

They whom we loved and lost so long ago
Dwell in those cities, far from mortal woe,
Haunt those fresh woodlands, whence sweet
    carolings soar.
    Eternal peace have they;
    God wipes their tears away;
They drink that river of life which flows for
    evermore.

June 20

Some twenty years ago, Professor Ezra Abbot made a list of authors who had treated of the future life and of their books. It contained between five and six thousand names and titles. If we could have all the books that have ever been written on it, and all the sermons and all the poems, like the stars in heaven for multitude, we should still have no adequate expression of the interest humanity has taken in this theme. For this interest antedates the earliest literary expression by hundreds and thousands of years. Before the invention of the first rude alphabet, a ruder faith in immortality had stirred the savage heart alike with hope and fear.

John W. Chadwick.

Nought we know dies. Shall that alone
    which knows
Be as a sword consumed before the sheath by
    sightless lightning?

Percy Bysshe Shelley.

June 21

A little while, and every fear
   That o'er the perfect day
Flings shadows dark and drear
   Shall pass like mist away;
The secret tear, the anxious sigh,
   Shall pass into a smile;
Time changes to eternity, —
   We only wait a little while.

                    Greville.

The purple stream which through my vessels
    glides
Dull and unconscious flows like common
    tides;
These pipes, through which the circling juices
    play,
Are not that thinking I, — no more than they;
This frame, compacted with transcendent
    skill,
Of moving joints obedient to my will,
Nursed from the fruitful glebe like yonder tree,
Waxes and wastes: I call it mine, not me.

June 22

What is the ground ye tread
But a mere point, compared with that vast
    space
  Around, above you spread,
  Where, in the Almighty's face,
The present, future, past, hold an eternal
    place?

  List to the concert pure
Of yon harmonious, countless worlds of light;
  See in his orbit sure
  Each takes his journey bright,
Led by an unseen hand through the vast maze
    of night.

Complain not that the way is long, — what
    road is weary that leads there? —
But let the angel take thy hand, and lead thee
    up the misty stair,
And then with beating heart await the open-
    ing of the golden gate.

Adelaide A. Proctor.

June 23

The progress of science is revealing to us the successive ages of the immeasurable past. That in the future there are to be successive ages or dispensations, the language of the Bible would declare, if it were not deprived of a true and full utterance. Of the theories of the future which exclude such ages, Dr. Tayler Lewis well says: "What a narrow idea, that the great antepast and the great future, after this brief world or olam has passed away, are to be regarded as having no chronology of a higher kind, no other time-worlds and worlds of worlds, succeeding each other in number and variety inconceivable!" As things are, heaven is looked on as a finished world, in which there is nothing that fires the imagination to be done in all the vast, the immeasurable ages of the coming future.

Edward Beecher.

June 24

Thou knowest not now; for here we see but
    darkly
  The outlines of his grace.
The rest is learned in heaven's eternal glory,
  And face to face.

Then thou shalt know: that passionless here-
    after
  Shall solve all mystery.
Dream not that life can hold the tide of
    wonder
  In store for thee.

  Still we say as we go,
  Strange to think by the way;
  Whatever there is to know,
  That shall we know some day.
        Dante Gabriel Rossetti.

June 25

I wait,
Till in white death's tranquillity
Shall softly fall away from me
This weary life's infirmity;
That I, in larger light, may learn
The larger truth I would discern,
The larger love for which I yearn.

I wait !
The summer of the soul is long;
Its harvests yet shall round me throng
In perfect pomp of sun and song.
In stormless mornings yet to be,
I 'll pluck from life's full-fruited tree
The joy to-day denied to me.

Mary Clemmer.

June 26

It is not necessary to be great ourselves to know that the great natures of the earth have been believing natures. Even you and I can remember that music, poetry, art, philosophy, literature, nay physics itself, owe something to faith. It is not easy to forget that Beethoven, Mozart, Bach, Handel, Haydn, Milton, Dante, Wordsworth, Raphael and Michael Angelo, Plato and Immanuel Kant and Leibnitz, Goethe and Shakespeare, Kepler and Newton, were believers in the existence of God, and the immaterial nature and immortal destiny of the human spirit.

Elizabeth Stuart Phelps Ward.

Science has given us a past. Too long has she left it to faith to give us a future. Human love cannot be counted out of the forces of nature; and earth-bound human knowledge turns to lift its lowered eyes toward the firmament of immortal life.

June 27

Not care to be immortal? Have you ever loved, have you ever thought, have you ever worshiped, and can yet say this? I *do* care for it. Prove to me that I have no reason to believe in it, or hope for it, and I will bear my fate as best I can. But I can never cease to care for it.

I have known men and women whose real death was an unthinkable proposition; as much so as a square circle, or the meeting of two parallel lines. Might not our own be so to us, if we should live the truest and divinest life we know? — *John W. Chadwick.*

Oh, wherefore sigh for what is gone,
   Or deem the future all a night?
From darkness through the rosy dawn
   The stars go singing into light.

And to the pilgrim lone and gray,
   One thought shall come to cheer his breast:
The evening sun but fades away
   To find new morning in the west.
          Thomas Buchanan Read.

June 28

We are sure at this moment that somewhere among the meadows or forests of this
planet, or down on the moist floor of the sea,
there is one narrow, pathetic spot of earth
eventually to become sacred with the deposit
of our mortal dust. One chamber there is
to-day, somewhere beneath an unrecognized
roof, that is by and by to grow august and
solemn with the entering-in of the inevitable
shadow. But neither that doom nor that
tomb can forcibly hold the disembodied spirit
for an hour. "Man dieth and wasteth
away;" but there yet remains the question,
"Where is he?"

It is not in the body that our immortality
resides; hence the shattering of the outward
semblance of a man has no effect whatever
upon the indefeasible and inalienable perpe-
tuity of the affections. "Your heart shall live
forever;" that heart is YOURSELF.

Charles S. Robinson.

June 29

Is it not sweet to think hereafter,
    When the spirit leaves this sphere,
Love, with deathless wings, shall waft her
    To those she long hath mourned for here?
Hearts from which 't was death to sever,
    Eyes this world can ne'er restore,
There, as warm, as bright as ever,
    Shall meet us and be lost no more.

Moore.

I shall awake as into Godhead born,
And with a fresh, undaunted soul arise,
Clear as the blue convolvulus at morn.

Helen Gray Cone.

Eternal form shall still divide
The eternal soul from all beside,
And I shall know him when we meet.

Alfred Tennyson.

June 30

The life of earth now, the life of heaven by-and-by, — each clear with its own glory. And our humanity capable of both, — capable of sharp thinking, timely hard work here and now, capable also of the supernal, the transcendent splendor there when the time shall come. — *Phillips Brooks.*

But souls that of his own good life partake
He loves as his own self; dear as his eye
They are to Him.   He'll never them forsake;
When they shall die, then God himself shall
      die;
They live, they live to all eternity.
                 Henry More.

The spiritual body is but the Visibility of the soul. — *Amiel.*

July 1

At these moments, when the earth seems fullest of beauty, one feels most strongly that it is but the harbinger of something else,— that the ceaseless play of Phenomena is no mere sport of Titans, but an orderly scene with its reason for existing, its —

> "One far-off divine event
> To which the whole creation moves."

John Fiske.

As tender mothers guiding baby steps,
   . . . lift up the little ones in arms
Of love, and set them down beyond the harm,
So did Our Father watch the precious boy,
Led o'er the stones by me, who stumbled of
Myself, but strove to help my darling on:
He saw the sweet limbs faltering, and saw
Rough ways before us, where my arms would
     fail;
So reached from heaven, and, lifting the dear
     child,
Who smiled in leaving me, He put him down,
Beyond all hurt, beyond my sight, and bade
Him wait for me! Shall I not, then, be glad,
And, thanking God, press on to overtake?

Helen Hunt.

July 2

Lord, thou hast let thy little ones in peace
     depart;
Thou sentest angels down to bear them where
     thou art;
Their spirits at the Gates of Glory didst re-
     ceive.
Forgive us that in places desolate we grieve.
Thy loving Spirit leads them up the holy hill,
And through the pastures green, beside the
     waters still.
There birds continually do sing, and flowers
     fair
Ne'er fade away, so sweet and pleasant is the
     air. . . .
They waited not the coming of life's flood-
     tide:
The world, with all its hurtful things, they left
     untried.
We thank thee we could give them back just
     as they came
Into our arms from thine, — white souls,
     without a stain.

Susan Teall Perry.

July 3

When the apple-tree blossoms, you laugh; and you do not cry when you pick the apple. But when man blossoms, man laughs; and then, when God picks the fruit, he cries. Why, your child is not your child until you have lost him. No bird cries when the shell is broken and the birdling comes forth, or when, a little later, it leaves the nest, and wings its way through the air. Only mothers do that when their children, released from earth, fly away to a better world.

How few there are who feel that, from the time the door of life opens and a child is born, God has drawn his hand out from near his own heart, and lent something of himself to the parent and said, " Keep it till I come : take this my own child, and educate it for me, and bring it to heaven !" It is a very solemn thing to have children, of which you are not only the parent, but the guardian and the guide, and in some sense the savior.

Henry Ward Beecher.

July 4

"Only a Baby's Grave."
    Some foot or two, at the most,
        Of star-daisied sod.
        Yet I think that God
    Knows what that little grave lost.

"Only a Baby's Grave."
    Will the little life be much
        Too small a gem
        For his diadem
    Whose Kingdom is made of such?

"Only a Baby's Grave."
    Strange how we mourn and fret
        For the little face
        That was here such a space:
    Oh, more strange could we forget!

"Only a Baby's Grave."
    Yet often we come and sit
        By the funeral stone,
        And thank God to own
    We are nearer Heaven for it.

July 5

Most parents, said the late Secretary Henry Kendall, are bereaved parents. Perhaps about one half of the human race live to become parents, and a majority of these encounter the enormous strain which attends this form of bereavement. This obviously enters as a very important element into the plans of God for shaping the lives and characters of his earthly children, and preparing them for Heaven. Bereaved parentage enables those so disciplined to appreciate better the nature of the atonement, to make which God spared not his own Son. Those who die early escape much trial, lose perhaps much discipline; yet possibly gain large advantages of which we know not. — *S. W. Boardman, D. D.*

God cannot have formed his intellectual creatures to break like bubbles and be no more. — *Blanco White.*

July 6

God took thee in his mercy
A lamb untasked, untried;
He fought the fight for thee,
He won the victory,
And thou art sanctified.

Now, like a dew-drop shrined
Within a crystal stone,
Thou 'rt safe in heaven, my dove!
Safe with the source of love,
The Everlasting One.

And when the hour arrives
From flesh that sets me free,
Thy spirit may await,
The first at Heaven's gate
To meet and welcome me.

Caroline Bowles Southey.

July 7

No one can tell why a child that is promising and virtuous, and in whom centre the hopes of the parent, should be taken before it has grown up. There is in human philosophy no answer to these questions that can satisfy the heart. The only reply that can be made to them is, that the branch that is broken here will have its full growth there; that children whose life is cut short in this world will have a new life under better auspices in the world to come; that what we lose on this side of the grave, we shall have again when we reach the other side. There comes in a larger sense of life. There comes in a thought of expansion and opening.

. . . .

It is hard to lose your children; therefore consecrate them, that they may never be lost.
Henry Ward Beecher.

July 8

Our hopes of thee were lofty,
    But have we cause to grieve?
Oh, could our fondest, proudest wish
    A nobler fate conceive?
The little weeper, tearless,
    The sinner, snatched from sin;
The babe to more than manhood grown
    Ere childhood did begin.

And I, thy earthly teacher,
    Would blush thy powers to see;
Thou art to me a parent now
    And I a child to thee!
Our God to call us homeward
    His only Son sent down:
And now still more to tempt our hearts
    Has taken up our own.

Thomas Ward.

July 9

I believe that we shall know our children as I believe that they shall know us. Will they not have grown? Very likely: I do not know; I cannot say. One thing I believe, and that is, that faith, hope and love are not relative. All that in my children which contained the seed of promise, all that which made them my companions and my joy,— that shall abide and shall be mine. They will not appear as they did in their mortal bodies. Their bodies will then be rare and exquisite compared with those which they wore on earth. But there will be lineaments by which I shall identify them.

Henry Ward Beecher.

"I supposed that heaven was dear to me; that my Father was there, and my friends were there, and that I had a great interest in heaven, but I *had no child there;* now I have: and I never think and never shall think of heaven, but with the memory of that dear child who is to be among its inhabitants forever."

July 10

It is a beautiful belief
That ever round our head
Are hovering on noiseless wing
The spirits of the dead.
It is a beautiful belief
When ended our career,
That it will be our ministry
To watch o'er others here; . . .
To bid the mourner cease to mourn,
The trembling be forgiven;
To bear away from ills of clay
The infant to its heaven.

Father, we *will* be comforted!
Thou wast the gracious giver:
We yield her up — not dead, not dead —
To dwell with thee forever!
Take thou our child!   Ours for a *day*,
Thine while the ages blossom!
This little shining head we lay
In the Redeemer's bosom!

July 11

A poor wayfarer, leading by the hand
A little child, had halted by the well
To wash from off her feet the clinging sand,
And tell the tired boy of that bright land
Where, this long journey passed, they longed
      to dwell.

When lo! the Lord, who many mansions had,
Drew near and looked upon the suffering
      twain,
Then pitying spake, " Give me the little lad;
In strength renewed and glorious beauty clad,
I'll bring him with me when I come again."

Did she make answer selfishly and wrong—
"Nay, but the woes I feel he too must share"?
Oh, rather bursting into grateful song,
She went her way rejoicing, and made strong
To struggle on, since he was freed from care.

July 12

Gone, gone from us! And shall we see
Those sibyl leaves of destiny,
Those calm eyes, nevermore?
Those deep, dark eyes so warm and bright,
Wherein the features of the man
Lay slumbering in prophetic light
In characters a child might scan?
So bright, and gone forth utterly!
O stern word — Nevermore!

.   .   .   .

Full short his journey was; no dust
Of earth unto his sandals clave;
The weary weight that old men must,
He bore not to the grave.
He seemed a cherub who had lost his way
And wandered hither, so his stay
With us was short, and 't was most meet
That he should be no delver in earth's clod,
Nor need to pause and cleanse his feet
To stand before his God:
O blest word — Evermore.

James Russell Lowell.

July 13

Those who have lost an infant are never, as it were, without an infant child. They are the only persons who, in one sense, retain it always, and they furnish other parents with the same idea. The other children grow up to manhood and womanhood and suffer all the changes of mortality. This one alone is rendered an immortal child.

Leigh Hunt.

He was so meshed within our love
That all our heartstrings bleeding lie
And all fond hopes we round him wove
    Are now but agony.
Yet let us suffer; he is freed,
And on our tears a bridge of light
Is built by God, his steps to lead
To joys beyond our sight.

William Wetmore Story.

July 14

Mother, I see you, with your nursery light,
Leading your babies, all in white,
      To their sweet rest ;
Christ the Good Shepherd carries mine to-
      night,
      And that is best.

You tremble each hour because your arms
Are weak : your heart is wrung with alarms,
      And sore opprest.
My darlings are safe out of reach of harms,
      And that is best.

You know over yours may hang even now
Pain and disease, whose fulfilling slow
      Naught can arrest ;
Mine in God's gardens run to and fro,
      And that is best.

Helen Hunt.

July 15

There stands our child before the throne
In royal vesture dressed;
A victor ere he drew the sword,
Ere he had toiled, at rest.
No doubts this blessed faith bedim,
We know that Jesus died for him.

Oh, blessed be the hand that gives,
Still blessed when it takes.
Blessed be He who smites to save,
Who heals the heart He breaks.
Perfect and true are all his ways,
Whom heaven adores and earth obeys.

July 16

Why should we weep or mourn, angelic boy,
For such thou wert ere from our sight re-
        moved,
Holy, and ever dutiful — beloved
From day to day with never ceasing joy,
And hopes as dear as could the heart employ
In aught to earth pertaining? Death has
            proved
His might, nor less his mercy as beloved —
Death conscious that he only could destroy
The bodily frame. That beauty is laid low
To moulder in a far-off field of Rome;
But heaven is now, blest child, the Spirit's
        home:
When such divine communion, which we
        know,
Is felt, thy Roman burial place will be
Surely a sweet remembrance of thee.

William Wordsworth.

July 17

And when I awake, I shall awake satisfied. I shall awake to a nobler and a better service. I do not know what it is, and yet I cannot but think it will be the service of love; ministering to the loved ones upon the earth. " His angels are ministering servants." What better ministering servant can the child have than the mother? What better ministering servant the mother than the child? They who have gone from us are with Christ, and we are with him, and so we are not far apart.

Lyman Abbott.

Never mother smiled
Like her who smiles forever, seeing one
Immortal child, for whom immortal father-
    hood
Beseeches and receives eternal good.

Helen Hunt.

July 18

I cannot tell what form is his, what looks he
    weareth now,
Nor guess how bright a glory crowns his shin-
    ing seraph brow.
The thoughts that fill his sinless soul, the bliss
    which he doth feel,
Are numbered with the secret things which
    God will not reveal.
But I know (for God hath told me this) that
    he is now at rest
Where other blessed infants be on their Sav-
    iour's loving breast.
I know the angels fold him close beneath
    their glittering wings,
And soothe him with a song that breathes of
    Heaven's divinest things.
I know that we shall meet our babe (his
    mother dear and I)
Where God for aye shall wipe away all tears
    from every eye.

John Moultrie.

July 19

When the baby died,
    On every side
Swift angels came in shining, singing bands,
And bore the little one with gentle hands
Into the sunshine of the spirit lands.
And Christ the Shepherd said
    Let them be led
In gardens nearest to the earth.
One mother weepeth over birth,
Another weepeth over death:
In vain all Heaven answereth.
Laughs from the little ones may reach
    Their ears, and teach
Them what, so blind with tears they never
    saw —
That of all life, all death, God's love is law.
                                    Helen Hunt.

July 20

I cannot make him dead !
His fair sunshiny head
Is ever bounding round my study chair ;
Yet when my eyes, now dim
With tears I turn to him,
The vision vanishes — he is not there !

. . . .

The grave, that now doth press
Upon that cast-off dress
Is but his wardrobe locked ; — he is not there.
He lives !   In all the past
He lives ; nor to the last
Of seeing him again will I despair ;
In dreams I see him now ;
And on his angel brow
I see it written, *Thou* shalt see me *there !*
Yes, we all live to God.
Father, thy chastening
So help us, thine afflicted ones, to bear,
That in the spirit land,
Meeting at thy right hand,
'Twill be our heaven to find that — he is
     there !

John Pierpont.

July 21

We wreathed about our darling's head
    The morning-glory bright.
Her little face looked out beneath,
    So full of love and light;
So lit as with a sunrise,
    That we could only say,
She is the morning-glory true,
    And her poor types are they.

The morning-glory blossoming
    Will soon be coming round —
We see their rows of heart-shaped leaves
    Upspringing from the ground;
The tender things the winter killed
    Renew again their birth,
But the glory of our morning
    Has passed away from earth.

Oh earth! in vain our aching eyes
    Stretch over thy green plain!
Too harsh thy dews, too gross thine air
    Her spirit to sustain.
But up in the groves of Paradise
    Full surely we shall see
Our morning-glory beautiful
    Twine round our dear Lord's knee.

July 22

I fancy my ardent, eager little boy as having some such employments in his new and happy home as he had here. I see him loving Him who took children in His arms and blessed them, with all the warmth of which his nature is capable, and as perhaps employed as one of those messengers whom God sends forth as his ministers. For I cannot think of those active feet, those busy hands as always quiet. — *E. Prentiss.*

We need not fear for them the coming winter's
    cold,
Nor summer's noontide heat : they 're in thy
    sheltered fold.
Nor need we watch with anxious eyes, at close
    of day,
Lest in the gathering darkness they might
    lose their way.

July 23

She is not dead, the child of our affection, —
But gone unto that school
Where she no longer needs our poor protection
And Christ himself doth rule.

In that great cloister's stillness and seclusion,
By guardian angels led,
Safe from temptation, safe from sin's pollution,
She lives whom we call dead.

Day after day we think what she is doing
In those bright realms of air;
Year after year her tender steps pursuing
Behold her grown more fair.

Thus do we walk with her and keep unbroken
The bond which nature gives,
Thinking that our remembrance though un-
spoken
May reach her where she lives.

Henry Wadsworth Longfellow.

July 24

One short and happy year
Thou smiledst on us below;
We hoped to keep thee here
Till we were called to go;
But God takes back the blessing lent,
Though we our weaker claims present.

To thee it was not given
To speak with mortal tongue;
The dialect of heaven
Already hast thou sung.
Too hard our speech — too slow our ways,
Angels must teach thee words of praise.

What we cannot discern
Thine eyes can plainly see;
How much have we to learn,
If we would equal thee.
Thine infant spirit near the throne
Excels all mind that earth hath known.

Dudley Phelps.

July 25

Let not then the death of your children
cause any inconsolable grief. The loss of
children, did I say — nay, let me recall so
harsh a word. The children we count lost
are not so. The death of our children is not
the loss of our children. They are not lost,
but given back; they are not lost, but sent
before. — *Cotton Mather.*

" Be — rather than be called — a child of
      God,"
  Death whispered; with assenting nod,
  Its head upon its mother's breast,
  The baby bowed without demur;
  Of the kingdom of the blest
  Possessor — not inheritor.
              Samuel Taylor Coleridge.

July 26

Beneath the sunny autumn sky
With gold leaves dropping round,
We sought, my little friend and I,
The consecrated ground,
Where calm beneath the holy cross,
O'ershadowed by sweet skies,
Sleeps tranquilly that youthful form.
Around the soft green swelling mound
We scooped the earth away,
And buried deep the crocus bulbs
Against a coming day.
These roots are dry and brown and sere,
Why plant them here, he said,
To have them all the winter long
So desolate and dead?
Dear child, within each sere dead form,
There sleeps a living flower,
And angel-like it shall arise
In spring's returning hour.
Ah, deeper down, cold, dark and chill,
We buried our heart's flower,
But angel-like shall he arise
In spring's immortal hour.

July 27

Of all his bright and winning ways
　No tongue or pen could tell:
But in the shortness of the days
　We learned to love them well.

But he was far too fair a flower
　To bloom till close of day;
With sunshine came to fill an hour,
　Was wafted far away.

His mission ended?　Brighter far
　The mission he is filling.
Though to our eyes he 's but a star,
　To follow him we' re willing.

" To hope in God " our motto be,
　He knoweth what is best.
The empty crib we clearly see;
　And, waiting, learn the rest.

A. M.

July 28

There was an idle lyre
  Amid Heaven's choral band;
A messenger was summoned
  To hear his Lord's command,
That from earth's lowly children
  Some favored one he bring,
Who had a skillful finger
  To sweep the golden string.

Some calm and saintly spirit?
  Some affluent soul whose praise
Hath caught the sacred key-note
  That seraph voices raise?
Some pure unearthly nature, —
  Some listening heart that hears,
In golden-centred silence,
  The music of the spheres?

A little child was playing
  Beside his mother's knee,
Clad in the simple meekness
  Of infant purity:
The angel smiling beckoned,
  And breathed the soft behest;
The lowliest one could waken
  The silent lyre the best.

To us this grave, to her the rows
The mystic palm-trees spring in;
To us the silence in the house;
To her the choral singing.
For her to gladden in God's view;
For us, to hope and bear on.
Grow, Lily, in thy garden new,
Beside the Rose of Sharon!

Grow fast in heaven, sweet Lily clipped,
In love more calm than this is,
And may the angels dewy-lipped
Remind thee of our kisses;
While none shall tell thee of our tears, —
These human tears now falling,
Till after a few patient years
One home shall take us all in.

Elizabeth Barrett Browning.

July 30

There is nothing — no, nothing innocent or good — that dies and is forgotten. An infant, a prattling child, dying in its cradle, will live again in the better thoughts of those who loved it, and will play its part through them in the redeeming actions of the world. There is not an angel added to the Host of Heaven but does its blessed work on earth in those that loved it here.

Forgotten! Oh, if the good deeds of human creatures could be traced to their source, how beautiful would even death appear; for how much charity, mercy and purified affection would be seen to have their growth in dusty graves!

July 31

Oh, it is beautiful!   Lifted so high, —
Up where the stars are, — into the sky,
Out of the fierce dark grasp of pain,
Into the rapturous light again!

Whence do ye bear me, shining ones,
Over the dazzling paths of suns?
Wherefore am I thus caught away
Out of my mother's arms to-day?

Baby-spirit, whose wondering eyes
Kindle, ecstatic with surprise,
This is the ending of earthly breath, —
This is what mortals mean by death.

Far in the silences of the blue,
See where the splendor pulses through;
Thither, released from a world of sin,
Thither we come to guide thee in:

In through each sevenfold circling band, —
In where the white child-angels stand, —
Up to the throne, that thou may'st see
Him who was once a babe like thee.

Margaret J. Preston.

August 1

It is a strengthening, calming consideration that we are in the midst of an invisible world of energetic and glorious life, a world of spiritual beings. . . . Blessed be God for the knowledge of a world like this. It is evidently that region or condition of space in which the departed find themselves immediately after death; probably it is nearer than we imagine, for St. Paul speaks of our being surrounded by a cloud of witnesses. There, it seems to me, they are waiting for us.

Canon Wilberforce.

Build thee more stately mansions, O my soul,
　As the swift seasons roll.
　Leave thy low-vaulted past;
Let each new temple, nobler than the last,
Shut thee from heaven with a dome more vast,
　Till thou at length art free,
Leaving thine outgrown shell by life's unresting sea.

Oliver Wendell Holmes.

August 2

But mark! The sun goes radiant to his goal,
While winds make music o'er the laughing
       sea;
And, with his set, the starry host will roll
Celestial splendors over mead and main;
Lord! Can thy worlds be glad, and death en-
       chain?
Nay! 't is but crowning for immortal reign,
In the pure realm where all abide with thee.

What star has seen the sun at cloudless noon?
What chrysalis knows aught of wings that
       soar? —
O blessed souls! How can I hope the boon
Of look or word from you, the glorified,
Until for me the shining gates swing wide?
Welcome the day when the great deeps divide,
And we are one in life for evermore!

Edna D. Proctor.

August 3

Still must the body starve our souls with shade;
But when Death makes us what we were be-
fore,
Then shall her sunshine all our depths invade,
And not a shadow stain heaven's crystal floor.
James Russell Lowell.

As thrills of long-hushed tone
Live in the viol, so our souls grow fine
With keen vibration from the touch divine
Of noble natures gone.
James Russell Lowell.

August 4

Two possessions we shall carry with us into the unseen: they are free of death and inalienable — one is character, the other is capacity. Is this capacity to be consigned to idleness and wantonly wasted? It were unreason: it were almost a crime. How this or that gift can be utilized in the other world is a vain question, and leads to childish speculation. We do not know where the unseen universe is, nor how it is constituted, much less how it is ordered, but our reason may safely conclude that the capacity which is exercised under one form here will be exercised under another yonder.

Ian Maclaren.

" Will the future life be work,
Where the strong and the weak, this world's
   congeries,
  Repeat in large what they practiced in small,
Through life after life in unlimited series,
  Only the scales be changed, that 's all ? "

Robert Browning.

August 5

We walk in a world where no man reads
   The riddle of things that are, —
From a tiny fern in the valley's heart
   To the light of the largest star, —
Yet we know that the pressure of Life is hard
   And the silence of Death is deep,
As we fall and rise on the tangled way
   That leads to the gate of Sleep.

We know that the problem of Sin and Pain,
   And the passions that lead to crime,
Are the mysteries locked from age to age
   In the awful vault of Time —
Yet we lift our weary feet and strive
   Through the mire and mist to grope
And find a ledge on the mount of Faith
   In the morning land of Hope.

August 6

To think that almost within the reach of the arm, separated from us by scarcely a hand's-breadth, is a realm where all goodness springs up spontaneously, and without obstruction; where all the body's hindrances, as well as helps, shall be laid aside; where aches and pains and losses and troubles shall be unknown; where lower temptations which take hold of us through the portals of the flesh shall be done away; and where everything that is gracious, and pure, and true, and beautiful in manhood shall lift itself up as the plants in the tropics lift themselves toward the sun, that "mortality might be swallowed up of life,"—to think of this is enough to wean one from the world. Who that does think of it, does not long for the world to come? — *Henry Ward Beecher.*

August 7

The Master commits five talents to the servant and the trust is shrewdly managed. The five become ten, and the Master is fully satisfied. What reward does He propose for his servant? Is it a release from labor and responsibility — a future in contrast with the past? No, the past shapes the future, and this servant, having served his apprenticeship, becomes himself a master — ruler over many things. So he entered into the joy of his Lord, and the joy for which Jesus endured the Cross is a patient and perpetual ministry. Life will be raised, not reversed; work will not be closed, it will be emancipated. The fret will be gone, not the labor; the disappointment, not the responsibility. Our disability shall be no more: our capacity shall be ours forever, and so the thorns shall be taken from our crown.

Ian Maclaren.

August 8

Multitudes, multitudes, stood up in bliss,
   Made equal to the angels, glorious, fair;
With harps, psalms, wedding-garments, kiss of
      peace,
   And crowned and haloed hair.

  .   .   .   .

As though one pulse stirred all, one rush of
   blood
   Fed all, one breath swept through them
     myriad-voiced,
They struck their harps, cast down their
   crowns, they stood
   And worshiped and rejoiced.

Each face looked one way like a morn new-
   lit,
   Each face looked one way towards the Sun
     of Love;
Drank love and bathed in love and mirrored it,
   And knew no end thereof.
             Christina G. Rossetti.

August 9

Life does seem sometimes a hard thing to bear, and all that makes it bearable is to occupy the mind with the nobler moods of contemplation; not shutting our eyes to what is mean and ugly, but striving to interpret it rightly. However we explain it, whether as implanted by God, or the result of long and laborious evolution, there is something in the flesh that is superior to the flesh; something that can in finer moments abolish matter and pain, and it is to this we must cleave. I do not see how even the loss of mind tells against a belief in this superior thing — for is the mind really dying in the same way the body dies? or is it only that the tools it works with are worn out or bent or broken? — *Lowell.*

Like the bird be thou,
That for a moment rests
Upon the topmost bough;
He feels the branch to bend
And yet as sweetly sings,
Knowing that he hath wings.
Victor Hugo.

August 10

The star is not extinguished when it sets
    Upon the dull horizon; but it goes
To shine in other skies, then reappear
    In ours, as fresh as when it first arose.
          Horatius Bonar.

       Our life's floor
Is laid upon eternity; no crack in it
But shows the underlying heaven.
          Charles Kingsley.

    All that is at all
    Lasts ever, past recall.
Earth changes, but thy soul and God stand
      sure.
          Robert Browning.

    The unseen world is not another place —
but another view.
          Immanuel Kant.

August 11

From a Letter. — I cannot feel, I do not feel, that —— has left us. I stand expectant, as one sometimes in summer stands waiting for a bird to begin his song again, and does not know that it has flown out of the tree. But I am conscious that I have transferred that dear and bright soul to the realms above. I do not mean precisely to heaven in the technical sense, but to everything toward which my thoughts move. Nature to me takes hue and color from every one who has gone; and the spirit seems to have mingled in such a sense with the universe, that it presents itself from every element, wherever I may turn my thoughts, for God took him. I do not wonder. And he is with God, and where is God not! . . . I cannot talk about him. It is in silence that he seems nearest. Memory is rich. He was one who was and is more than Memory can set forth. . . . We are moving toward him. Every day the wheels turn faster. Our dear ones will soon stand at the gate to receive us, and we shall look back with wonder on our grief. — *Beecher.*

August 12

Round us on every side are cramped, hindered, still-born lives — merchants who should have been painters, clerks who should have been poets, laborers who should have been philosophers. Their talent is known to a few friends; they die, and the talent is buried in their coffin. Jesus says No, it has at last been sown for the harvest; it will come into the open and blossom in another land. These also are being trained — trained by waiting. They will get their chance; they will come into their kingdom —

> "Where the days bury their golden suns
> In the dear hopeful West."

Ian Maclaren.

August 13

If we could know — somewhat as John must have known after his vision — the presence of God into which our friend enters on the other side, the higher standards, the larger fellowship with all his race and the new assurance of personal immortality in God; if we could know all this, how all else would give way to something almost like a burst of triumph as the soul which we loved went forth to such vast enlargement, to such glorious consummation of its life. — *Phillips Brooks.*

Earth may not pass till Heaven shall pass
    away,
   Nor heaven may be renewed
Except with earth; and once more in that day
   Earth shall be very good.
              Christina G. Rossetti.

August 14

How shall I know thee in the sphere that
    keeps
  The disembodied spirits of the dead,
When all of thee that time could wither sleeps
  And perishes among the dust we tread?

Will not thine own meek heart demand me
    there —
  That heart whose fondest throbs to me were
    given?
My name on earth was ever on thy prayer:
  Shall it be vanished from thy tongue in
    heaven?

The love that lived through all the stormy
    past,
  And meekly with my harsher nature bore,
And deeper grew, and tenderer to the last, —
  Shall it expire with life and be no more?
              William Cullen Bryant.

August 15

For none return from those quiet shores,
Who cross with the boatman cold and pale;
We hear the dip of the golden oars,
And catch a gleam of the snow-white sail, —
And lo! they have passed from our yearning
    heart;
·They cross the stream and are gone for aye;
We may not sunder the veil apart
That hides from our vision the gates of day.

.   .   .   .

And I sit and think, when the sunset's gold
Is flushing river, and hill, and shore,
I shall one day stand by the waters cold,
And list for the sound of the boatman's oar;
I shall watch for the gleam of the flapping
    sail,
I shall hear the boat as it gains the strand;
I shall pass from sight, with the boatman pale,
To the better shore of the spirit land;
I shall know the loved who have gone before,
And joyfully sweet will the meeting be,
When over the river, the peaceful river,
The angel of death shall carry me.

Nancy A. W. Priest.

August 16

"The loved and lost!" Why do we call
    them lost?
Because we miss them from our onward road?
God's unseen angel o'er our pathway crost,
Looked on us all, and loving them the most,
Straightway relieved them from life's weary
    load.

They are not lost; they are within the door
That shuts out loss, and every hurtful thing—
With angels bright and loved ones gone be-
    fore,
In their Redeemer's presence evermore,
And God himself their Lord and Judge and
    King.

And this we call a "loss;" oh, selfish sorrow
Of selfish hearts. Oh, we of little faith!
Let us look round some argument to borrow
Why we in patience should await the morrow
That surely must succeed this night of death.

August 17

Doth it not cast a nameless charm around an early death, to consider how entirely hidden from a child are all the black spots in this world of sin? They have never been bound down by the iron chain of habit. Nor have they encountered temptations demanding a constant warfare. Are they not then qualified for a different mission in the economy of the kingdom of heaven and for holding a different place in the glorified company? May we not suppose that their Father in heaven, who early transplants so many of these little ones thither, has some special design to serve — some work for them in his house above — "for of such is the kingdom of heaven?"

The Way Home.

"How beautiful to be with God!"
Miss Willard's last words.

August 18

What is it if we die, whose eyes have seen
There is no death.   What is it if we live
A little woebegone when He hath passed
Patiently all our path, changing its stones
To rubies, and to rose blooms all its thorns,
With bright blood of his vainly-wounded
      feet?

  Jesus taught
Life beyond this life, timeless, infinite;
As little parted from the world we see
As daytime is from dreamtime, when we
      drowse
And think 't is night, with sunrise on our lids.
                Edwin Arnold.

August 19

Ask the poor sailor when the wreck is done
Who with his treasures strove the shore to
    reach,
While with the raging waves he battled on,
Was it not joy where every joy seemed gone,
To see his loved ones landed on the beach?

We will do likewise: death hath made no
    breach
In love and sympathy, in hope and trust;
No outward sign or sound our ears can reach,
But there's an inward, spiritual speech,
That greets us still, though mortal tongues be
    dust;

It bids us do the work that they laid down —
Take up the song where they broke off the
    strain;
So journeying till we reach the heavenly town,
Where are laid up our treasures and our
    crown,
And our lost loved ones will be found again.

August 20

They whom God sent us, robed in sacred
    light,
        Out of his sky,
With snow and roses, stars and sunbeams
    bright —
Too beautiful they must be in his sight
        Ever to die.

Out of the years bloom the eternities;
        From earth-clogged root
Life climbs through leaf and bud by slow de-
    grees
Till some far cycle heavenly blossoms sees,
        And perfect fruit.

And nothing dies that ever was alive;
        All that endears
And sanctifies the human must survive;
Of God they are, and in his smile they
    thrive —
        The immortal years.

August 21

O strong soul, by what shore
Tarriest thou now ?   For that force,
Surely, has not been left vain !
Somewhere, surely, afar,
In the sounding labor-house vast
Of being, is practiced that strength
Zealous, beneficent, firm !

Yes, in some far shining sphere,
Conscious or not of the past,
Still thou performest the word
Of the spirit in whom thou dost live,
Prompt, unwearied as here.
Still thou upraisest with zeal
The humble good from the ground,
Sternly repressest the bad.
Still like a trumpet dost rouse
Those who with half open eyes
Tread the border-land dim
Twixt vice and virtue ; revivest,
Succorest — this was thy work,
This was thy life on earth.

Matthew Arnold.

August 22

It follows upon Jesus' suggestion of the next life — the continuation of the present on a higher level — that it will be itself a continual progress, and Jesus gives us frequent hints of this law. When He referred to the many mansions in his Father's house, He may have been intending rooms — places where those who have been associated together on earth may be gathered together; but He may be rather intending stations — stages in that long ascent of life that shall extend through the ages of ages. In the parable of the unjust steward Jesus uses this expression in speaking of the future, " everlasting tents." It is at once a contradiction and an explanation, for it combines the ideas of rest and advance — a life of achievement where the tent is pitched, a life of possibilities where it is being forever lifted. — *Ian Maclaren.*

August 23

God! do not let my loved one die,
But rather wait until the time
That I am grown in purity
Enough to enter thy pure clime,
Then take me, I will gladly go
So that my love remain below.

Oh, let her stay! She is by birth
What I through death must learn to be;
We need her more on our poor earth
Than thou canst need in heaven with thee.
She hath her wings already, I
Must burst this earth-shell ere I fly.

Then, God, take me! We shall be near,
More near than ever, each to each:
Her angel ears will find more clear
My heavenly than my earthly speech:
And still, as I draw nigh to thee
Her soul and mine shall closer be.

James Russell Lowell.

August 24

My love, I have no fear that thou shouldst die;
Albeit I ask no fairer life than this,
Whose numbering clock is still thy gentle kiss
While Time and Peace with hand enlockèd fly;
Yet care I not where in Eternity
We live and love, well knowing that there is
No backward step, for those who feel the bliss
Of faith as their most lofty yearnings high.
Love hath so purified my being's core
Meseems I scarcely should be startled even
To find some morn that thou hadst gone be-
       fore;
Since with thy love this knowledge too was
       given,
Which each calm day doth strengthen more
       and more,
That they who love are but one step from
       Heaven.

James Russell Lowell.

And they that be wise shall shine as the brightness of the firmament; and they that turn many to righteousness as the stars forever and ever. — *Daniel* 12 : 3.

August 25

Jesus heartens his followers by an assurance that not one hour of labor, not one grain of attainment, not one honest effort on to the moment when the tools of earth drop from their hands, but will tell on the after life. Again one is tempted to quote the sagacious Taylor. "All the practical skill we acquire in managing affairs, all the versatility, the sagacity, the patience and assiduity, the promptitude and facility, as well as the highest virtues which we are learning every day, may well find scope in a world such as is rationally anticipated when we think of heaven as the stage of life which is next to follow the discipline of life." — *Ian Maclaren.*

August 26

Let Death possess thy body,
Thy soul is still with me,
More sunny and more gladsome
Than it was wont to be:
Thy body was a fetter
That bound me to the flesh —
Thank God that it is broken,
And now I live afresh.
Now I can see thee clearly
The dusky cloud of clay
That hid thy starry spirit
Is rent and blown away.
To earth I give thy body,
Thy spirit to the sky,
I saw its bright wings growing
And knew that thou must fly.
James Russell Lowell.

Some people's bodies get so tired that they
long for the rest of the grave; it is my soul
that gets tired, and I know the grave can give
that no rest; I look for the rest of more life,
more strength, more love.
George Macdonald.

August 27

Now I can love thee truly,
For nothing comes between
The senses and the spirit,
The seen and the unseen :
Lifts the eternal shadow,
The silence bursts apart,
And the soul's boundless future
Is present in my heart.

Therefore thy hope
May yet not prove unfruitful, and thy love
Meet day by day with less unworthy thanks,
Whether, as now, we journey hand in hand,
Or, parted in the body, yet are one
In spirit and the love of holy things.
                    James Russell Lowell.

August 28

I cannot say, and I will not say
That he is dead.   He is just away.

Think of him passing on, as dear
In the love of There as the love of Here;
Think of him still as the same.   I say :
He is not dead — he is just away !
                              James Whitcomb Riley.

" We are as near heaven by sea as by land."
Last words of Sir Humphrey Gilbert before
his vessel foundered off Cape Breton.

Look up and behold the eternal fields of
light that lie round about the throne of God.
Had no star ever appeared in the heavens, to
man there would have been no heavens; and
he would have laid himself down to his last
sleep in a spirit of anguish, as upon a gloomy
earth vaulted over by a material arch — solid
and impervious. — *Jean Paul Richter.*

August 29

If any of the priests and prophets of the materialistic philosophy had been told fifteen years ago, while they sat precipitating our soul into a sub-acetate in their laboratories, or offering us little icicles from the Glacial Period to replace the Easter lilies on the new-made grave, that more than one of the foremost scientists of Great Britain would be to-day avowed believers in the psychical nature of obscure phenomena, such as it has been hitherto considered good intellectual form to turn over to the juggler and the medium, — but imagination cannot struggle beyond the learned smile with which such a suggestion would have been bowed out.

John W. Chadwick.

This life is but the cradle of the other. What avail then sickness, time, old age, death — different degrees of a metamorphosis which doubtless has here below only its beginning?

Joubert.

August 30

Weep not, beloved friends! nor let the air for
     me
With sighs be troubled.   Not from life
Have I been taken; this is genuine life
And this alone — the life which now I live
In peace eternal: where desire and joy
Together move in fellowship without end.
    Wordsworth, translated from Chiabrera.

There shall the good stand in immortal bloom
   In the fair gardens of that second birth;
And each bright blossom mingle its perfume
   With that of flowers which never bloomed
     on earth.
    Henry Wadsworth Longfellow.

August 31

My Comforters. — Yea, why not mine?
The power that kindled you doth shine,
In man a mastery divine;

That Love which throbs in every star,
And quickens all the worlds afar,
Beats warmer where his children are.

The shadow of the wings of Death
Broods over us; we feel his breath;
" Resurgam " still the spirit saith.

These tired feet, this weary brain?
Blotted with many a mortal stain,
May crumble earthward — not in vain.

With swifter feet that shall not tire,
Eyes that shall fail not at your fire,
Nearer your splendors I aspire.

Edward Rowland Sill.

September 1

It is always a sad day to me in autumn when I see the change that comes over nature. Along in August the birds are all still, and you would think there were not any left; but, if you go out into the fields, you find them feeding in the trees, and hedges, and everywhere. By and by September comes, and they begin to gather together in groups; and anybody that knows what it means, knows that they are getting ready to go. And then come the later days of October, — the sad, the sweet, the melancholy, the deep days of October. And the birds are less and less. And in November, high up you see the sky streaked with water-fowl going southward; and strange noises in the night, of these pilgrims of the sky, they shall hear whose ears are attuned to natural sounds. Birds in flocks, one after another, wing their way to the South. Summer is gone, and I am left behind; but they are happy. And I think I can hear them singing in all those States clear down to the Gulf. They have found where the sun is never cold. With us are frosts, but not with the bird that has migrated. — *H. W. Beecher.*

September 2

Do they remember who have passed death's
      portals,
The friends they loved on earth in days gone
      by;
There in the blessed land of the immortals,
The yearning faces left beneath the sky?

And if remembering, how can they be joyous,
Even in that land where sorrow is unknown;
Nor even hear amid the heavenly chorus,
Earth's heart-breaks mingling their sad under-
      tone?

We love enough to spare the loved one trial,
God loves enough to send the needed pain,
The cross, the suffering, the self-denial,
The earthly loss that brings eternal gain.

So must it be, that dwelling there so near Him,
Knowing the joy that from our pain must come,
Our loved ones wait, knowing that they shall
      hear Him
In his good time say, "Weary ones, come
      home."

Wakefield.

September 3

The souls of the righteous are in the hands of God : their hope is full of immortality.

Immortality is not a doctrine of Christianity alone. It belongs to the Human Race. You may find nations so rude that they live houseless, in caverns of the earth; nations that have no letters, not knowing the use of bows and arrows, fire, or even clothes, but no nation is without a belief in immortal life.

Theodore Parker.

Jesus explained nothing, but the influence of Him took people out of time and they felt eternity. — *Ralph Waldo Emerson.*

September 4

All is not lost that's passed beyond our keeping.
Sight is not gone though eyes be dim with
  weeping;
Sweet voices still are sounds of love repeating,
Though heavy ears scarce catch the tones re-
  treating.

Brief is the space that from our loved divides
  us,
Thin is the mist that from their haven hides us;
Soft hands on high are beckoning signals
  holding,
White arms wait patient for our heart's en-
  folding.

There all, and always, dwell within his keeping
Who sleepless careth, while our care is sleeping;
How can we dare to falter in our praying,
Their perfect bliss against our sorrow weighing?

September 5

I cannot think of death as more than the going out of one room into another. . . . The world of imagination is the world of eternity. It is the divine bosom into which we shall all go after the death of the vegetated body. This world of imagination is infinite and eternal; whereas the world of generation or vegetation is finite and temporal. There exist in that eternal world the permanent realities of everything which we see reflected in this vegetable glass of nature. — *William Blake.*

He himself passed mild and majestical,
Through Death's black gate, whose inner side
    none saw
Before He set it wide, golden and glad,
Conqueror for us of the unconquerable.
Edwin Arnold.

September 6

Where the blessed are, is heaven; but whether it is near or far, whether it is above or below, we know not.

I believe that I shall know my friends, and that they will know me, in heaven. I know that we shall be as the angels of God; I know that we shall be satisfied, because we shall be like him; I know that we shall be sons of God, but it doth not yet appear what that shall be. Nobody can now tell what that means. I shall know you, but it will be in your coronation robes. It will be when you have on your crowns, not of silver or of gold, but of a glorious, heavenly, divine virtue. It will be when you shall bear the palm, not of any perishing tree, but of immortalities gathered in you. — *Henry Ward Beecher.*

September 7

I feel conscious of Immortality; that I am not to die — no, never to die, though often to exchange. I cannot believe this desire and consciousness are felt only to mislead, to beguile, to deceive me. I know God is my Father, and the Father of the Nations. Can the Almighty deceive his children? For my own part, I can conceive of nothing which shall make me more certain of my Immortality. — *Theodore Parker*.

The Chaldeans, with no pretense to miraculous inspiration, taught the idea of Immortality.

The Egyptians believed in the immortality of the soul, four thousand years before the birth of Christ. — *A. Wiedermann*.

To me the eternal existence of my soul is proved from my idea of activity. — *Goethe*.

September 8

The mists of death hang low upon life's sea,
  The unseen shore
Beyond the darkness rises silently
  Forevermore;
The golden city flashes from the strand,
But mortal eye sees not the distant land.

But there are voices in that unseen land
  Which we have heard,
Of loved ones standing with us, hand in hand,
  With smile and word
That kindled here our hearts with friendship's
  glow
And breathed on us their music sweet and low.

And there are souls that thrill with love etern
  Who look on Him
For whom the stars in endless lustre burn;
  Where seraphim
Delighted bask around the throne of light
In ceaseless wonder at the infinite.

Anon.

September 9

We knew them here and with them wept and
     smiled,
        Our life was one;
We met and parted, still of each beguiled;
        Their work is done;
And they are resting in the morning land
And we are toiling yet with heart and hand.

We group them oft in visions of the soul,
        A joyous band,
As on the peaceful hills of light they stroll
        In that fair land;
Or wander on the shore with loving gaze,
To watch the comers from the dark sea haze.

Speed on, my bark, life's stormy sea across,
        The mists will rise;
And every pain and tear and earthly loss
        In strange surprise
Shall vanish when the unseen shore shall greet
Thine eye and thou shalt touch the golden
     street.

Anon.

September 10

There is in man's nature that which makes him susceptible to the tremendous idea of unending existence as an attribute of his own spirit.

> "Here sits he, shaping wings to fly,
> His heart forebodes a mystery —
> He names the name Eternity."
>
> *Philip S. Moxom.*

With his eye pressed to the telescope that his own genius has invented, he penetrates illimitable space, and studies the star so remote that its light has sped through millenniums before it reaches his pedestal, the earth, and yet as Parker says, "the biggest star is at the little end of the telescope." — *Moxom.*

September 11

If we suppose, in accordance with the belief of the great majority, that the real man is not identical with his body, but only its inhabitant and ruler; the presumption that his conscious being ends with the destruction of the body falls at once. — *C. A. Young.*

There is much in the discoveries of psychic science not only to support and strengthen the belief in immortality, but to convert that belief into knowledge. — *Elliot Coues.*

After mature reflection, it seems to me that science has nothing whatever to say on the question. The only basis of our faith in Immortality must be found in Revelation.
President A. P. Barnard.

September 28

The period of time is brief,
'T is the red in the red rose leaf,
'T is the gold of a sunset sky,
'T is the flight of a bird on high;
But one may fill the space
With such an infinite grace
That the red shall vein all time,
And the gold through the ages shine,
And the bird fly swift and straight
To the portals of God's own gate.

Thou art not idle; in thy higher sphere
Thy spirit bends itself to loving tasks,
And strength to perfect what it dreamed of
       here
Is all the crown of glory that it asks.

Lowell's Elegy to Channing.

September 13

The spirit's ladder
That from this gross and visible world of dust,
Even to the starry world with thousand rounds
Builds itself up; on which the unseen powers
Move up and down on heavenly ministries —
The circles in the circles that approach
The central sun with ever narrowing orbit.

Samuel Taylor Coleridge.

There is no reason to think that God will destroy the soul — He who destroys not the least atom in the Universe; there is no reason to think He will destroy it at the moment when He separates it from the body than at any other time, since it is an existence foreign to the body and independent of it. It is rather the deliverance and release of the soul, and not the cause of its destruction. — *Fénelon.*

October 16

How many weary sufferers blessed the hand
Which knew so well a healing balm to pour,
While hungry voices never were denied
By her who kept as steward a poor man's store!
E'en death is powerless o'er a life like hers;
Its radiance lingers though its sun is set.
Rich and unstinted was the seed she sowed;
The golden harvest is not gathered yet.

   The last look at destiny is that of a seat in
the eternal throne; all limitation ended, all
heights surmounted, all things hoped and
waited for gained. — *T. T. Munger.*

October 17

I held his letter in my hand,
  And, even when I read,
The lightning flashed across the land
  The word that he was dead.

How strange it seems! His living voice
  Was speaking from the page
These courteous phrases tersely choice,
  Light-hearted, witty, sage.

I wondered what it was that died!
  The man himself was here,
His modesty, his scholar's pride,
  His soul serene and clear.

These neither death nor time shall dim :
  Still this sad thing must be, —
Henceforth I may not speak to him,
  Though he can speak to me.

Thomas Bailey Aldrich.

October 18

Resignation is the courage of old age; it will grow in its own season, and it is a good day when it comes to us. Then there are no more disappointments; for we have learned that it is even better to desire the things that we have than to have the things that we desire. And is not the best of all our hopes — the hope of immortality — always before us? How can we be dull or heavy while we have that new experience to look forward to? It will be the most joyful of all our travels and adventures. It will bring us our best acquaintances and friendships. But there is only one way to get ready for immortality, and that is to love this life, and live it as bravely and cheerfully and faithfully as we can.

Henry Van Dyke.

October 19

Tears are often the telescope through which we behold the invisible.

So it is often with the bravest and best. What is Death to them, that they should say his litany? Do we stop to cower and tremble before the outside portal of our Father's mansion? Straight on, straight in, with the same step that we have always walked. O death, where is thy sting? O grave, where is thy victory? — *Garret*.

After the shower the tranquil sun;
Silver stars when the day is done.

October 20

And so he died; and, so dying, he well-nigh changed my grief into rejoicing, so completely did the sight of his happiness overpower the recollection of my own misery. O Lord, thou hast but called thine own, thou hast but taken what belonged to thee. And now my tears put an end to my words. I pray thee teach me to put an end to my tears.

Bernard of Clairvaux.

There is a calm the poor in spirit know,
That softens sorrow and that sweetens woe;
There is a peace that dwells within the breast
When all without is stormy and distrest;
There is a Light that gilds the darkest hour,
When dangers thicken and when tempests
     lower.
That calm to faith and hope and life is given;
That peace remains when all beside is risen;
That light shines down to man direct from
     heaven.

October 21

It must be very terrible. The Saviour's words, in his sense of loneliness amidst the crowd, and even amidst his own disciples, will be full of meaning to you : " I am not alone, for the Father is with me." But for that, the universe would have been a wilderness to this heart. Our human hands are too coarse to meddle with the fine network of the spirit. We break and confuse oftener than we harmonize and heal. But He can do it ! and with what wisdom, patience, tenderness, and holy love ! Oh, what a mockery it would be if our social life in Christ ended here ! It hardly begins here ! Very soon you and your sister will meet ; and when you talk over old times, you may be able to praise and bless God for this time, now so dark and trying. Most certain it is that God, by such trials, when we wait on Him, trust Him, and seek his kingdom, will purify us, and make us instruments more fit to glorify Him.

Norman MacLeod.

October 22

Ther is lyf withoute ony deth,
And ther is youthe without ony elde;
And ther is alle manner welthe to welde:
And ther is rest without ony travaille;
And ther is pees without ony strife,
And ther is alle manner lykinge of lyf:—
And ther is bright somer ever to se,
And ther is nevere wynter in that countrie:—
And ther is more worshipe and honour,
Than evere hade kynge other emperour.
And ther is grete melodie of aungeles songe,
And ther is preysing hem amonge.
And ther is alle manner frendshipe that may be,
And ther is evere perfect love and charite;
And ther is wisdom without folye,
And ther is honeste without vileneye.
Al these a man may joyes of hevene call;
Ac yutte the most sovereyn joye of alle
Is the sighte of Godde's bright face,
In wham resteth alle mannere grace.

> *Richard Rolle.*   About 1350.

October 23

Thomas Hood loved all nature like a child, and possessed that rare faculty of enjoyment which even a clear day or a beautiful flower can bring to a finely sensitive mind. He said once to us: " It 's a beautiful world, and since I have been lying here I have thought of it more and more; it is not bad, even humanly speaking, as people would make it out. I have had some very happy days while I lived in it, and I could have wished to stay a little longer. But it is all for the best, and we shall all meet in a better world."

And we may surely humbly believe that —

" Another life-spring there adorns
    Another youth, without the dread
Of cruel care, whose crown of thorns
    Is here for manhood's aching head.
Oh, there are realms of welcome day,
A world where tears are wiped away!
    Then be thy flight among the skies:
Take, then, oh, take the skylark's wing,
    And leave dull earth, and heavenward rise
O'er all its tearful clouds, and sing
    On skylark's wing!' '

October 24

Mr. Standfast said: "This river has been a terror to many; yea, the thoughts of it also have often frightened me. Now, methinks, I stand easy; my foot is fixed upon that on which the feet of the priests that bare the ark of the covenant stood, while Israel went over this Jordan. The waters, indeed, are bitter to the palate, and to the stomach cold; yet the thoughts of what I am going to, and of the conduct that waits for me on the other side, doth lie as a glowing coal at my heart." Now, while he was thus in discourse, his countenance changed; his strong man bowed under him; and, after he had said, "Take me, for I am come unto thee," he ceased to be seen of them.

But glorious it was to see how the open region was filled with horses and chariots, with trumpeters and pipers, with singers and players on stringed instruments, to welcome the pilgrims as they went up, and followed one another in at the beautiful gate of the city. — *John Bunyan.*

October 25

Death's decree is supreme. He disdains all the barriers that rank and station, fame and fortune, can erect for their protection. He holds a secret key to every dwelling. Still, the dread of death comes from our imperfect and partial view of life. All momentary griefs are nothing more than mere dots of darkness in a vast expanse of light. The universe is one glowing, boundless field of life, in which every death chamber is an anteroom of the infinite temple, and every death scene a triumphal hour of entrance through an arch of shadow into eternal day.

Raleigh wrote these lines on the fly-leaf of his Bible shortly before his death : —

"Even such is Time, that takes on trust
Our youth, our joys, and all we have,
And pays us but with age and dust;
Who in the dark and silent grave,
When we have wandered all our ways,
Shuts up the record of our days.
Yet from this earth, this grave, this dust,
The Lord shall raise me up, I trust."

October 26

When Bishop Butler lay on his death-bed he called for his chaplain and said: "Though I have endeavored to avoid sin, and to please God, to the utmost of my power; yet, from the consciousness of perpetual infirmities, I am still afraid to die." "My lord," said the chaplain, "you have forgotten that Jesus Christ is a Saviour." "True," was the answer, "but how shall I know that he is a Saviour for me?" "My lord, it is written, 'Him that cometh to me I wjll in no wise cast out.'" "True," said the bishop, "and I am surprised that, though I have read that Scripture a thousand times over, I never felt its virtue till this moment; and now I die happy."

Twenty years before, and how often since, Charles Kingsley had expressed his longing for the moment of death: "God forgive me if I am wrong, but I look forward to it with an intense and reverent curiosity." And he said to his dying wife: "It is not darkness you are going to, for God is light. It is not lonely, for Christ is with you. It is not an unknown country, for Christ is there."

October 27

So pray we, when our feet draw near
The river, dark with mortal fear,

And the night cometh, chill with dew,
O Father, let thy light break through!

So let the hills of doubt divide;
So bridge with faith the sunless tide;

So let the eyes that fail on earth
On thy eternal hills look forth;

And in thy beckoning angels know
The dear ones whom we loved below.

Whittier.

Side by side, for the way was one,
The toilsome journey of life was done,
And all who in Christ the Saviour died
Came out alike on the other side.
No forms, or crosses, or books had they;
No gowns of silk, or suits of gray;
No creeds to guide them, or MSS.,
For all had put on Christ's righteousness.

Mrs. Cleveland.

October 28

But they do come and go continually,
Our blessed angels, no less ours than his;
The blessed angels whom we think we miss;
Whose empty graves we weep to name or see,
And vainly watch, as once in Galilee
    One, weeping, watched in vain
    Where her lost Christ had lain.

Whenever in some bitter grief we find,
All unawares, a deep, mysterious sense
Of hidden comfort come, we know not
      whence;
When suddenly we see, where we were blind;
Where we had struggled, are content, resigned;
    Are strong where we were weak, —
    And no more strive nor seek, —

Then we may know that from the far, glad
      skies,
To note our need, the watchful God has bent,
And for our instant help has called and sent,
Of all our loving angels, the most wise
And tender one, to point to us where lies
    The path that will be best,
    The path of peace and rest.

October 29

With each new inch added to the diameter of the telescope, millions of starry worlds rush into sight. Thus, with each new endowment for the soul, new ranges of the world of truth and beauty pass before man's vision. Here man carries very imperfect instruments for knowing. He is but a seed to be grave-planted. That would be but an ignoble immortality, and an impoverished futurity, that man could understand. Even the poet, the sage, and the seer discern but hints and gleams of the infinite truth and beauty awaiting all. Happily for us, the future of our race is inconceivably beyond anything man can discern by the utmost strength of reason or imagination. — *N. D. Hillis.*

There were scattered hopes of the immortality of the soul, especially among the Jews. The Romans never received it. The Greeks never reached it. There were intimations, crepuscular twilight; but, but, but God in the Gospel of Jesus Christ, brought life and immortality to light. — *Daniel Webster.*

October 30

Life's race well run,
Life's work all done,
Life's victory won :
　Now cometh rest.

Sorrows are o'er,
Trials no more,
Ship reacheth shore :
　Now cometh rest.

Faith yields to sight,
Day follows night,
Jesus gives light :
　Now cometh rest.

We a while wait ;
But, soon or late,
Death opes the gate :
　Then cometh rest.

E. H. P.

October 31

I believe most seriously that death is a crisis in our spiritual history. I believe that it is an important and tremendous crisis. Unrobing the spirit of the flesh; lifting it out from connection with the world in which it may have taken ignoble and unholy pleasure; striking away from it the cushion of its sloth, the banquets of its transitory delight, the channels of its vice, the pleasant draperies with which it has curtained itself against the calls of duty; setting it face to face with the splendors of truth, for which its untrained eye is weak, before the blaze of holy realities, and within the grasp of laws whose majesty it has slighted, but which it sees now in all their severity and grandeur; unloosing it, a weak and faithless spirit, it may be, in a spiritual world the alphabet of whose language it refused, perhaps, to learn in the flesh, — I dare not tell you that I think this will be anything less than a mighty and tremendous crisis for you and for me. All easy and volatile raptures about passing from this world into the next, as though then all care is over and peace is sure, sound to me not only weak but repulsive. — *Starr King*.

November 1

I shall find them again, I shall find them again,
    Though I cannot tell when or where ;
My earthly own, gone to worlds unknown,
    But never beyond Thy care.

   .   .   .   .

Only at times through our soul's shut doors
    Come visits divine as brief,
And we cease to grieve, crying, " Lord, I be-
        lieve,
    Help Thou mine unbelief."

Linger a little, invisible host
    Of the sainted dead who stand
Perhaps not far off, though men may scoff —
    Touch me with unfelt hand.

Ah, they melt away, as the music dies,
    Back comes the world's work, — hard,
        plain ;
Yet God lifted in grace the veil from his face,
    And it smiled, " Thou shalt find them
        again."

                      D. M. Craik.

November 2

Creation hangs as a veil, woven over senses
and spirits, over the Infinite and the eternities;
pass by before the veil, and draw it not away
from the splendor which it hides.

Jean Paul Richter.

Up above where stars are gleaming
Lies the heaven of which we 're dreaming
And the joy which earth denies.

Heine.

I die in the belief of only one God, the
Creator of the world, whose pity I implore
for my immortal soul. — *From Heine's Will.*

November 3

Blessed be God for the gathering in and eternal union of his people. Our friends in heaven remain the same persons with all their sinless peculiarities. They therefore remember us and love us more than ever. Are they interested in us? perhaps concerned about us? Why not? The joy of the redeemed is not a selfish joy. I would despise the saint who enjoyed himself in a glorious mansion, singing psalms, and who did not wish his joy disturbed by sharing Christ's noble and grand care about the world. So long as man and my dear ones are in the " current of the heady flight," I don't wish to be ignorant of them on the ground that it would give me pain and mar my joy. I prefer any pain to such joy.

The soul on earth is an immortal guest,
Compelled to starve at an unreal feast :
A spark, which upwards tends by nature's
      force ;
A stream diverted from its parent source ;
A drop dissevered from the boundless sea ;
A moment parted from eternity.
Hannah More.

November 4

I cannot think it possible that my heaven there shall be different from my heaven here, which consists in sympathy with Christ. If He has a noble anxiety limited by perfect faith in what is going on upon earth, if human sin is a reality to Him, if his life there as well as here is by faith in the Father, if He watches for the end, and feels human sin and sorrow, and rejoices in the good, and feels the awfulness of the wrong, yet ever has deep peace in God, why should not this people have the joy of sharing this God-like burden of struggling humanity? — *Norman MacLeod.*

Joy, shipmate, joy.
Pleased to my soul at death I cry,
Our life is closed, our life begins,
The long, long anchorage we leave,
The ship is clear at last, she leaps,
She swiftly courses from the shore.
Joy, shipmate, joy.
                    Walt Whitman.

November 5

If it should be that we are watched unaware
By those who are gone from us; if our sighs
Ring in their ears; if tears that scald our eyes
They see and long to stanch; if our despair

Fills them with anguish — we must learn to
       bear :
In strength of silence.   Howso doubt denies
It cannot give assurance which defies
All peradventure, and if anywhere

Our loved grieve with our grieving, cruel we
To cherish selfishness of woe.   The chance
Should keep us steadfast.   Tortured utterly,

This hope alone in all the world's expanse
We clutch forlornly : how deep love can be,
Grief's silence proving more than utterance.
                    Arlo Bates.

November 6

Is it so far? When those who have gone
    thither
Seem so near always, always near and sure,
Loving and abiding still, sharing our joy and
    ill,
Lifting our burdens, helping to endure.

Is it so far, then? I cannot believe it
When the veil parts and rends and lets us
    through,
The first surprise of bliss I think will be in
    this, —
That the far-off was nearer than we knew.

That which we mourned as lost was close be-
    side us,
Touching us every day in every spot,
While, blended with dull tears, groping thro'
    faithless years
We were upheld and led and knew it not!
Susan Coolidge.

November 7

It might be of use for the sincere doubters to engage in one strictly logical exercise. It is this : Let him accept the idea of annihilation and then follow out its relentless logical significance into all departments of personal life. . . . Let him try to live logically as a believer in annihilation; let it shape his idea of his relation to his friends, his children, and humanity at large; let it shape his thoughts about those whom death takes from his side,—and then, perhaps, when he experiences that devastating creed, clouding every sacred fellowship of life with the idea of speedy termination, and chilling every noble ardor of the soul with the irony of death, he might find in his bleak experience an argument, not indeed sufficient to create faith in eternal life, but strong enough to turn him toward the idea of it, with at least a desire that it might be true. And when that desire stirs in the soul, it is, I must think, the beginning of the spiritual nature which grows into the unshaken conviction that there is a life beyond the grave. — *Percy Browne.*

November 8

As the good and dear are buried out of your sight, as youth dies, as the years bear you on to trial and pain, you are carrying onward, if walking with the Master, more and more that shall bloom again and adorn your larger life when mortality is all swallowed up. And so, looking out on the opening season, on the faces of children that cling to you, and of friends that are true; thinking over the days of your vanished prime, and the joys which came so often in a loving service that you have not strength to render now, — you are not to grow sad, as if all that were gone forever, as if you were mocked by a loveliness that you could not keep, as if the kernel of existence were almost consumed, and soon all would be as if you had not been. No; you are not to look at things in this way, — you cannot, indeed, in the tender and unerring sympathy of Christ. The divine promises are all glorious of the hereafter. The instinct of the pious soul is to foreshadow the ages in the reaches of faith and affection.

H. N. Powers.

November 9

Could Abraham or Jacob, in their night watch under the Chaldean sky, have wrung from the pitying stars the secret of the Divine Name if they were to live scarcely longer than their bleating flocks? Can they who have once drunk at the immortal fountain of the Divine presence become a handful of dust, dry as the desert sands they used to cross? The love of the creature of a day could hardly reach to the Infinite and Eternal, and win his answering care; nor could the qualities of an atom " crushed before the moth " image to us the Power who is " from everlasting to everlasting." The fact, then, that men can know Him by faith is a proof of their immortality, for how could they know one to whom they were not akin? In that contact with God the soul is a partaker of the Divine Nature, and he is brought into such connection with the lives of men, that they must share his Infinite Life. All these considerations justify that strong word of Emerson, " I have always thought that faith in immortality was a proof of the sanity of a man's nature."

Henry W. Foote.

How little of ourselves we know,
Before a grief the heart has felt !
The lessons that we learn of love
May brace the mind as well as melt.

The energies too stern for mirth,
The strength of thought, the strength of will,
Mid cloud and tempest have their birth,
Through blight and blast their course fulfill.

And yet, 't is when it mourns and fears
The loaded spirit feels forgiven ;
And through the mist of falling tears
We catch the clearest glimpse of heaven.

Lord Maspeth.

November 11

The surest way to convince one's self that there is a life after death is so to act in the present that one must wish it.

J. G. Fichte.

All death in nature is birth, and at the moment of death appears visibly the rising of life. There is no dying principle in nature, for nature throughout is unmixed life, which, concealed behind the old, begins again and develops itself. Death and birth is simply the circling of life in itself, in order to present itself more brightly and like itself.

J. G. Fichte.

" That which thou sowest is not quickened except it die." — *St. Paul.*

November 12

When I am dead, strew flowers upon my grave ; but let no heathenish practice prevail at my funeral, — of putting on black drapery and the livery of sorrow for a soul which has passed through the shadow of death into eternal life. — *Henry Ward Beecher.*

She had expressed to me the feeling that our funerals were all too sad, and I have read the 103d Psalm in place of the one usually read, as it was her favorite, and expressed her more cheerful views of death. I must here appeal to you women once more, to cease draping everything with crape when friends are taken from our midst. — *Lyman Abbott.*

November 13

With brain o'erworn, with heart a summer
    clod,
With eye so practiced in each form around, —
And all forms mean, — to glance above the
    ground
Irks it, each day of many days we plod,
Tongue-tied and deaf along life's common
    road :
But suddenly, we know not how, a sound
Of living streams, an odor, a flower crowned
With dew, a lark upspringing from the sod,
And we awake.   Oh, joy of deep amaze !
Beneath the everlasting hills we stand,
We hear the voices of the morning seas
And earnest prophesyings in the land,
While from the open heaven leans forth at
    gaze
The encompassing great cloud of witnesses.
                Edward Dowden.

November 14

The blessed dead! how free from stain is our love for them! The earthly taint of our affections is buried with that which was corruptible, and the divine flame in its purity illumines our breast. We have now no fear of losing them. They are fixed for us eternally in the mansions prepared for our reunion. We shall find them waiting for us, in their garments of beauty. The glorious dead! how reverently we speak their names! Our hearts are sanctified by their words which we remember. How wise they have now grown in the limitless fields of truth! How joyous they have become by the undying fountains of pleasure! The immortal dead! how unchanging is their love for us! How tenderly they look down upon us, and how closely they surround our being! How earnestly they rebuke the evil of our lives.

November 15

How beautiful is the memory of the dead! What a holy thing it is in the human heart, and what a chastening influence it sheds upon human life! How it subdues all the harshness that grows up within us in the daily intercourse with the world! How it melts our unkindness, softens our pride, kindling our deepest love, and waking our highest aspirations! Is there one who has not some loved friend gone into the eternal world, with whom he delights to live again in memory? Does he not love to sit down in the hushed and tranquil hours of existence, and call around him the face, the form, so familiar and cherished — to look into the eye that mirrored not more clearly his own face than the soul which he loves — to listen to the tones which he loves to listen to, the tones which were once melody, and have echoed softly in his ear since they were hushed to his senses? .... Every year witnesses the departure of some one whom we knew and loved; and when we recall the names of all who have been near to us in life, how many of them we see passed into that city which is imperishable.

November 16

There are but two calms, — the calm of the grave and of heaven, — the rest of death, and of perfected life. To rest before the voyage is over is to miss the haven.

Mrs. Charles.

Closed eyes
That looked no thought of ill,
Ye ope after this little while
In Paradise.

Folded hands
That wrought no works but Christ's,
Now, knowingly ye fulfil
Your Lord's commands.

Beloved Soul
Prisoned in suffering flesh,
Now joyful thou dost live,
Freed and made whole.

A. R. B.

November 17

"Let men talk pleasantly of the dead, as those who no longer suffer and are tried — as those who pursue no longer the fleeting, but have grasped and secured the real. With them the fear and the longings, the hope, and the terror, and the pain are past : the fruition of life has begun. How unkind, that when we put away their bodies, we should cease the utterance of their names. The tender-hearted dead who struggle so in parting from us ! why should we speak of them in awe, and remember them only with sighing ? Very dear were they when hand clasped hand, and heart responded to heart. Why are they less dear when they have grown worthy a higher love than ours? . . . By their hearthside and by their grave-side, in solitude and amid the multitude, think cheerfully and speak lovingly of the dead."

"We die and disappear!
  Of myriads passed within the veil, but one
Has e'er returned the mystery to clear!
  He — God's incarnate Son!
Then was the dark obscure made bright,
  O'er Death and Grave the victory was won,
And life immortal brought to light!"

November 18

Not in the time of pleasure
    Hope doth set her bow,
But in the sky of sorrow,
    Over the vale of woe.

Through gloom and shadow look' we
    On beyond the years;
The soul would have no rainbow
    Had the eyes no tears.
                    John Vance Cheney.

        Have we not left
That grand impulse to every great endeavor
Which swathes the broken heart by partings
    cleft?
Hope, skyward, burns its beacon light forever,
Beckoning us toward the truth: this have we
    left
        Who are bereft.

November 19

There are two worlds, — one where we live for a short time, and which we leave never to return; the other, which we must soon enter, never to leave. Influence, power, friends, high fame, great wealth, are of use in the first world; the contempt of all these things is for the second. We must choose between the two. — *La Bruyère.*

The faith of immortality depends on a sense of it begotten, not on an argument of it concluded. — *Bushnell.*

I cannot believe, and cannot be brought to believe, that the purpose of our creation is fulfilled by our short existence here. To me, the existence of another world is a necessary supplement of this, to adjust its inequalities, and imbue it with moral significance.
Thurlow Weed.

Visiting spirits are near ;
They are not wholly silent, but we cannot
      hear
Nor understand their speech.
Our Saviour caught his Father's word,
And men of old, dreaming and walking, heard
The breathings of a world we cannot reach.

They mounted to the skies
And read deep mysteries,
While yet on earth they placed a ladder there
Like Jacob's, that each round should lead,
By prayer outspoken, in a word or deed,
The soul to heights of clearer, purer air.

They saw no messenger of gloom
In him whom we call Death,
Nor met their doom
As prisoner his sentence ; but naturally, as
      bud unfolds to flower,
As child to man, so man to angel,
They recognizing Death the glad evangel
Leading to higher scenes of life and power.

November 21

The ships sail out to sea bearing our beloved on errands of their own, yet we weep
when they drop below the rim of ocean and
are lost in the expanse. But the trailing
cloud of glory up yonder, where the heavens
touch the ground, is the chariot sent for them
who go on errands for the King, and find at
length the dividing of the ways where earth
is left and heaven found. Of course we
weep, but not as if the separation were of our
own choosing, nor as if the voyage might suffer
storm and wreck. For the grandest journey
a man can take, the most assured glory that
on any one can fall, the highest honor, the
best success, possible to any of our race, are
held up for our admiration and desire when a
true, good man goes hence to be with God.

Evangelist.

November 22

Truth is the same for all worlds. Reason and conscience affirm truth forever. Personal individuality is unimpaired. In heaven they are interested in the same great objects of thought as on earth. Character will continue. Adaptations to earth will pass away, but not holy love. Charity never faileth. Knowledge of truth is as real on earth as in heaven, though more limited. "Now I know in part, but then shall I know even as I am known." Service is the same in essence, though different in form. We are to set our affections on things above, but not to know them fully until we reach them. Personal identity and the mental faculties will endure forever. No creature could be judged, rewarded, or punished without intelligence and memory concerning the past earthly life for which he was judged. — *S. W. Boardman.*

Death is as necessary to the constitution as sleep : we shall rise refreshed in the morning.
Benjamin Franklin.

November 23

Builders with God are we to-day,
Building within our homes of clay
   The better home of the spirit;
High on the Mount He shows the plan
By which to build the heavenly man
   Of the graces we inherit.

Builders and heirs of God are we:
His the rich materials be,
   And his the mansions we rear;
Let us look to it well that all
Be builded so they may not fall   ˙
   When the tempests of life are near;

That when we drop the props of clay,
When the scaffolding falls away,
   The eternal structure fair to see
May in its due proportion stand,
Majestic, beautiful, and grand,
   Worthy of immortality.

November 24

The traveler, in passing up the west side of the Hudson in the cars, goes through a lovely country, where on every side he sees Nature in countless beautiful forms. Suddenly the train dashes into the dark tunnel and seems swallowed up. So the beautiful lives of the friends we treasure here pass on and seem lost in the Valley of the Shadow of Death. But beyond the tunnel the train emerges beside the grand river, and we find the darkness was but temporary, and rejoice as we shall also in the life beyond the grave. When we see the mountain stream dash into cavernous depths, disappearing from our view, none of us believe that it has ceased to exist. We know that somewhere it continues to flow on in its grand beauty. So the life of our friend we so tenderly loved has only passed through the darkness to live forever in the sunshine of God's presence. The separation causes us great sorrow ; but there is a separation, far worse than death, that is caused by sin. Let us take heed, mother, husband, children, and friends, that this comes not between us and those we love and honor. — *Lyman Abbott.*

November 25

The word "angel" does not indicate another order of being, but only a new *office* to which the spirits of men, redeemed and perfected, are exalted, — that of *messengers* and ministers of good to spirits and to man.

Throughout the Scriptures there are visions of angels and they are called men. Abraham "looked, and, lo! three *men* stood by him." They were angels. An angel met Jacob on his way, but it is said "there wrestled a *man* with him until the breaking of the day." When Joshua lifted up his eyes before Jericho, "lo and behold, there stood a man over against him," who declared himself to be "the captain of the Lord's host." When the angel appeared to Manoah's wife she said, "A *man* of God came unto me." The angel Gabriel, who was sent to Daniel, is called "the man Gabriel." The women at the sepulchre saw "*two young men* sitting" on the right side clothed in linen, while John says they were "angels." — *Rev. L. P. Mercer.*

November 26

God does not send us strange flowers every
    year
When the spring winds blow o'er the plea-
    sant places:
The same dear things lift up the same fair
    faces;
      The violet is here.

It all comes back, — the odor, face, and hue,
Each sweet relation of its life repeated;
No blank is left, no lurking foe is cheated:
    It is the thing we knew.

So after the death, — winter it must be.
God will not put strange signs in the hea-
    venly places;
The old loves shall look out from the old
    faces.
      Veilchen, I shall have thee!
          Mrs. Whitney.

November 27

He comes, a severe, sedate, immovable, dark rider, driving his truncheon of universal sway, as he passes along the lengthened line on the pale horse of the Revelation. It is Death! Who else could assume the guidance of a procession that comprehends all humanity? Beggars in their rags, and Kings trailing the regal purple in the dust; the Warrior's gleaming helmet; the Priest in his sable robe; the hoary Grandsire, who has run life's circle and come back to childhood, the ruddy Schoolboy with his golden curls, frisking along the march; the Artisan's stuff jacket; the Noble's star-decorated coat, — the whole presenting a motley spectacle, yet with a dusky grandeur brooding over it. Onward, onward! . . . And whither? We know not; and Death, hitherto our leader, deserts us by the wayside, as the tramp of our innumerable footsteps echoes beyond his sphere. He knows not, more than we, our destined goal. But God, who made us, knows, and will not leave us on our toilsome and doubtful march, either to wander in infinite uncertainty, or perish by the way! — *Hawthorne*.

November 28

Oh, ye seraphs of love and light !
Stay for a little your lofty flight;
Stay, and adown the star-sown track
Haste to my weeper, — haste ye back !

Tell her how filled and thrilled I am ;
Tell her how wrapt in boundless calm ;
Tell her I soar, I sing, I shine ;
Tell her the heaven of heavens is mine ! ''

Tenderest comforter, — Faith's own word,
Sweeter than ours, her heart hath heard ;
Softly her solaced tears now fall :
Christ's own whisper hath told her all !

Margaret J. Preston.

To me the darksome tomb
Is but a narrow room,
Where I may rest in peace from sorrow free.
Thy death shall give me power
To cry in that dark hour,
O Death, O Grave, where is your victory?

The grave can nought destroy,
Only the flesh can die,
And e'en the body triumphs o'er decay:
Cloth'd by thy wondrous might
In robes of dazzling light,
This flesh shall burst the grave at that last Day.

My Jesus, day by day,
Help me to watch and pray,
Beside the tomb where in my heart Thou 'rt laid.
Thy bitter death shall be
My constant memory,
My guide at last into Death's awful shade.

S. Franck, 1711.

I beheld, and, lo! a great multitude which no man could number, of all nations and kindreds and peoples and tongues, stood before the throne and before the Lamb, clothed with white robes and palms in their hands, saying:

"Salvation to our God which sitteth upon the throne and unto the Lamb."

What are these? And whence came they?

These are they which came out of great tribulation, and have washed their robes and made them white in the blood of the Lamb.

Rev. vii. 9–14.

December 1

The harvest fields lie bleak and brown
    Beneath December snows ;
There is no breath of violet,
    No fragrance of the rose ;
Of birds or brooks no roundelays, —
      O weary days !

Yet somewhere, in her sweet content,
    Spring waits God's loving call,
And sets her buds unquestioning,
    Since He is over all :
Beneath the snows that fall to-day,
      Sleep blooms of May !

O patient souls, storm-beat and driven,
    And robbed by wintry blast,
Who hold, through all God's chastening,
    His promises so fast,
Or soon or late his love shall bring
      Eternal spring !

Ellen E. Chase.

December 2

Those who have left us are still, through their influence, present and active among us. Their forms have vanished into the realm which our vision cannot pierce ; and we miss them — how sorely ! — from our empty and desolate lives. But they are with us. They are speaking to us still. Like angels of God, free from all earthly limitations, they come and go ; nay, rather, they come and do *not* go. They are near us all the time. We feel, and love to feel, their influence upon us, — the gathered influence of many years, now consecrated and clarified by death. It may seem to us in our sorrow as if there were nothing left to us of those whom we had cherished so tenderly. But no treasure that the world could offer would make us willing to part with that which still is ours, — the memories and the influences which will be, while our days go on, an element and an energy in our most secret life. — *E. B. C. Coe.*

December 3

Sorrow not as those without hope ;
What we call life is a journey to death ;
What we call death is a passport to life.
We should thank Death for what he takes,
And still more for what he gives.

I know not where His islands lift
  Their fronded palms in air ;
I only know I cannot drift
  Beyond His love and care.
      John Greenleaf Whittier.

I believe that no love, no life, goes ever
from us ; it goes, as He went, that it may
come again, deeper, clearer, and surer, and be
with us always, even to the end of the world.
      Mrs. A. D. T. Whitney.

December 4

How can one be certain that Jesus is with God? It is a question of the last importance. There are four lines of proof. The first is the reliable evidence that Jesus rose from Joseph's tomb: this is for a lawyer. The second is historical, the existence of the Christian Church: this is for a scholar. The third is mystical, — the experience of Christians: this is for a saint. The fourth is ethical, — the nature of Jesus' life: this is for every one. The last is the most akin to the mind of Jesus, who was accustomed to insist on the self-evidencing power of his life. He is alive because he could not die. "I am the Resurrection and the Life."

Ian Maclaren.

Immortality is the result created by our own degree of achievement in spirituality, and it is a varying and ever-progressive condition.

Kate Field.

December 5

To me " the crystal has shone faint between " souls here and there, the homes on earth and those above, and more and more the beloved who have ascended are those who mediate directly and sweetly between my soul and the Master's.

The " cloud of witnesses " not only makes life on earth a nobler thing, but heaven more glowing and alluring. — *Dr. Storrs.*

So poor the world, now they have gone,
We scarcely dare to think upon
The years before our rest is won.
But yet our Father knoweth best
The joy or sadness that we need ;
The time when we may take our rest,
And be from sin and sorrow freed.
So we will wait with patient grace
Till, in that blessed gathering place,
We meet our friends and see His face.

December 6

Oh, what a wondrous life is ours !
　To dwell within this earthly range,
Yet parley with the heavenly powers, —
　Two worlds in interchange !

O balm of grief ! to understand
　That those our eyes behold no more
Still clasp us with as true a hand
　As in the flesh before !

For what is our proof of immortality ? Not the analogies of nature, — the resurrection of nature from a winter grave, — or the emancipation of the butterfly. Not even the testimony to the fact of risen dead; for who does not know how shadowy and unsubstantial these intellectual proofs become in unspiritual frames of mind ? No; the life of the spirit is the evidence. Heaven begun is the living proof that makes the heaven to come credible. " Christ in you is the hope of glory." . . . He alone can believe in immortality who feels the resurrection in him already. — *F. W. Robertson.*

December 7

When I see the heavenly sun buried under earth in the evening of the day, and in the morning to find a resurrection to his glory, why (think I) may not the sons of heaven, buried in the earth in the evening of their days, expect the morning of their glorious resurrection? Each night is but the past day's funeral, and the morning his resurrection; why then should our funeral sleep be other than our sleep at night? Since then the glory of the sun finds a resurrection, why should not the sons of glory? Since a dead man may live again, I will not so much look for an end of my life as wait for the coming of my change. — *Arthur Warick.*

If pausing over some cherished dust, we recall the truth and beauty that once were associated with it, it is only that we may look thence into the future, where all sweet impulses shall be in perfect and perpetual bloom; that we may contrast the life, amid darkness and toil, that is past, with the life that is to come, dimly seen, far away, by the " delectable mountains."

December 8

And solemn before us,
Veiled the dark portal,
Goal of all mortal.
Stars, silent, rest o'er us, —
Graves under us, silent.

While earnest thou gazest
Comes boding of terror,
Come phantasm and error;
Perplexes the bravest
With doubt and misgiving.

But heard are the voices,
Heard are the sages,
The Worlds and the Ages :
" Choose well ; your choice is
Brief, and yet endless."

Here eyes do regard you
In Eternity's stillness ;
Here is all fullness,
Ye brave, to reward you.
Work, and despair not.

Goethe.

December 9

The desire to be remembered, after our life on earth is over, is one of the signs which exhibit the grandeur of the human soul, and is fruitful of great suggestions concerning its design and its destiny. Time holds us now, and we cannot altogether escape from the restraint which it imposes on our thought and our action. But we are greater than time, and eternity is the real measure of our life. The impulse which prompts us to make our personality a living force, if possible, among those who live after us, is at once a sign of the superiority of the soul to its present physical conditions, and is the instinct and the pledge of immortality. — *E. B. C. Coe.*

We shape ourselves the joy or fear
Of which the coming life is made,
And fill our future's atmosphere
With sunshine or with shade.
There shall the soul around it call
The shadows which it gathered here,
And, painted on the eternal wall,
The Past shall reappear.

December 10

The apostle calls the body a tabernacle or tent. When a tent is taken down, the removal of the boards or curtains will let in light quite new and different from what was seen before. Waller has borrowed this thought : —

> " The soul's dark cottage, battered and decayed,
>   Lets in new light through chinks that time has made."

We are surrounded with a great cloud of witnesses, and, though we cannot see them, I believe they see us. Before the moment of death, great discoveries have been made, and both the pious and the profane have strong intimations whither they are going, and with what company they soon will mingle. My dear daughter Eliza was a remarkable instance of this. She was still a child, but while the tent was taking down she appeared to see invisibles and to hear unutterables. . . . The earthly dwelling concealed the inhabitant within, and greatly restrained the exertion of her noblest powers.

Rev. John Newton.

December 11

So when the old delight is born anew,
And God reanimates the early bliss,
Seems it not all as one first trembling kiss,
Ere soul knew soul with whom she has to
      do ?
O nights how desolate, O days how few,
O death in life, if life be this, be this !
O weighed alone, as one shall win or miss
The faint eternity which shines therethro',
So all that age is as a speck of sand,
Lost on the long beach where the tides are
      free,
And no man metes it in his hollow hand,
Nor cares to ponder it, how small it be ;
At ebb it lies forgotten on the land,
And at full tide forgotten in the sea.

Frederic W. H. Myers.

December 12

To Victor Hugo, death was the laying aside of an old vesture for a finer robing, a promotion, a step upward, nothing more. On this point his intuitive perceptions were so pronounced as to leave him no room for doubt. They amounted to an absolute certainty, enabling him to confront the grave with a serene smile while he exclaimed : " I feel in myself the future life. I am like a forest which has been more than once cut down. The new shoots are stronger and livelier than ever. I am rising, I know, toward the sky. The sunshine is on my head. . . . Winter is on my head, and eternal spring is in my heart, when I breathe at this hour the fragrance of the lilacs, the violets, and the roses, as at twenty years. The nearer I approach the end, the plainer I hear around me the immortal symphonies of the woods, which invite me. It is marvelous yet simple. When I go down to the grave I can say, like many others, I have finished my day's work; but I cannot say I have finished my life. My day's work will begin the next morning.

December 13

How sweet it were if, without fright,
Or dying of the beauteous sight,
An angel came to us, and we could bear
To see him issue from the silent air
At evening, in our room, and bend on ours
His divine eyes, and bring us from his bowers
News of dear children who have never
Been dead indeed, as we shall know forever !
Alas !   We think not that we daily see,
About our hearths, angels that *are* to be,
Or may be if they will, and we prepare
Their souls and ours to meet in happy air;
A child, a friend, a wife, whose soft heart
        sings
In unison with ours, breeding its future wings.

Leigh Hunt.

December 14

What is it that leads us to attach the value we do to intellectual labor and achievement? — not the mere practical result of those engagements, nor the mere labor in itself considered; but the *emotion*, the sentiment, and the moral power connected with it, and by which it is prompted, animated, and rewarded. Within the entire circle of our intellectual constitution, we value nothing but emotion: it is not the powers, or the exercise of the powers, but the fruit of those powers, in so much *feeling*, of a lofty kind, as they will yield. Now, that toward which we are constantly tending as our goal, — that which we rest in when attained as sufficient, — it is that which shall be ultimate, and shall survive whatever has been mediate, or contributory, or accessory. Everything short of the affections of the soul is a means to an end, and must have its season: it is temporary; but the affections of the soul are the end of all, and they are eternal. Let the universe perish, or be changed, — the soul shall live.

Isaac Taylor.

December 15

Oh, deem not that earth's crowning bliss
   Is found in joy alone ;
For sorrow, bitter though it be,
   Hath blessings all its own.

From lips divine, like healing balm
   To heart oppressed and torn,
The heavenly consolation fell,
   " Blessed are they that mourn."

Who never mourned have never known
   What treasures grief reveals,
The sympathies that humanize,
   The tenderness that heals, —

The power to look within the veil
   And learn the heavenly lore,
The key-word to life's mysteries,
   So dark to us before.

Supernal wisdom, love divine,
   Breathed thro' the lips which said,
Oh, blessed are the souls that mourn, —
   They shall be comforted.
         William Henry Burleigh.

December 16

A year uncalendared ; for what
    Hast thou to do with mortal time ?
Its dole of moments entereth not
    That circle, infinite, sublime,
Whose unreached centre is the throne
    Of Him before whose awful brow,
Meeting eternities are known
    As but an everlasting *Now !*
The thought uplifts thee far away, —
    Too far beyond my love and tears ;
Ah, let me hold thee as I may,
    And count thy time by earthly years !

A year of tears to me ; to thee,
    The end of thy probation's strife,
The archway to eternity,
    The portal of thy deathless life ;
To me, the corse, the bier, the sod ;
    To thee, the palm of victory given.
Enough, my bruisèd heart ! Thank God
    That thou *hast* been a year in heaven !
               Margaret J. Preston.

December 17

Do we indeed desire the dead
   Should still be near us at our side?
   Is there no baseness we would hide,
No inner vileness that we dread?

Shall he for whose applause I strove —
   I had such reverence for his blame —
   See with clear eye some hidden shame,
And I be lessen'd in his love?

I wrong the grave with fears untrue:
   Shall love be blamed for want of faith?
   There must be wisdom with great Death:
The dead shall look me thro' and thro'.

Be near us when we climb or fall:
   Ye watch, like God, the rolling hours
   With larger other eyes than ours,
To make allowance for us all.

Tennyson.

December 18

The principle of life — that is to say, Mind — is not dissoluble by any other principle; nor can it give way before any intensity of a merely material energy; and, although doubtless dependent upon the pleasure of the Creator, and immortal only by his will who sustains that which He has produced, yet must it be thoroughly independent of all co-existent and inferior forces or powers. Let, then, the material universe vanish, silent and unnoticed as a dream; or let it melt with fervent heat and pass away, as in a painful struggle and convulsion, with a " great noise : " in either case all minds, rational and moral, shall emerge from the mighty ruin and float clear and untouched above the terrors and the tempest of Nature's dying day. Mind shall shake itself of the corruptible and dissoluble elements, and shall put on incorruption : it shall lay down the dishonor of its union with the inert masses of the material world, and put on the glory of a purely active and un-compounded corporeity ; it shall take leave of death, and be clothed with immortality.

Isaac Taylor.

December 19

Sunset and evening star,
    And one clear call for me!
And may there be no moaning of the bar
    When I put out to sea,

But such a tide as moving seems asleep,
    Too full for sound and foam,
When that which drew from out the boundless
        deep
    Turns again home.

Twilight and evening bell,
    And after that the dark!
And may there be no sadness of farewell
    When I embark;

For tho' from out the bourne of Time and
        Place
    The flood may bear me far,
I hope to see my Pilot face to face,
    When I have crost the bar.

Tennyson.

December 20

Speak, History! Who are Life's Victors? Unroll
   Thy long annals, and say
Are they those whom the world called the
   victors
   Who won the success of a day, —
The martyrs, or Nero? The Spartans who
   fell
   At Thermopylæ's tryst,
Or the Persians and Xerxes? His judges or
   Socrates?
   Pilate or Christ?

William Wetmore Story.

Deep in the heart of pain God's hand hath
   set
   A hidden rest and bliss;
Take as his gift the pain, the gift brings yet
   A truer happiness;
God's voice speaks through it all, the high
   behest
That bids his people enter into rest.

December 21

Let down the bars, O Death!
   The tired flocks come in,
Whose bleating ceases to repeat,
   Whose wandering is done.

Thine is the stillest night,
   Thine the securest fold;
Too near thou art for seeking thee,
   Too tender to be told.

A death-blow is a life-blow to some,
Who, till they died, did not alive become;
Who, had they lived, had died; but when
They died vitality began.

Emily Dickinson.

December 22

Moreover, those new materials and sur-
roundings of the farther being would bring a
more intense and verified as well as a higher
existence. Man is less superior to the sensitive plant now than his reëmbodied spirit
would probably then be to his present personality. Nor does anything, except ignorance
and despondency, forbid the belief that the
senses, so etherealized and enhanced, and so
fully adapted to fine combinations of an ad-
vanced entity, would discover, without much
amazement, sweet and friendly societies spring-
ing from, but proportionately upraised above,
the old associations. Art divinely elevated;
science splendidly expanding; bygone loves
and sympathies explaining and obtaining their
purpose; activities set free for vaster cosmic
service; abandoned hopes and efforts realized in rich harvests at last; despaired-of joys
come magically within ready reach; regrets
and repentances softened by wider knowledge,
by surer foresight, and by the discovery
that, although in this universe nothing can
be " forgiven," everything may be repaired
and repaid. — *Edwin Arnold.*

December 23

Oh listen, man !
A voice within us speaks the startling word,
" Man, thou shalt never die ! " Celestial
    voices
Hymn it around our souls ; according harps,
By angel fingers touched, when the mild stars
Of morning sang together, sound forth still
The song of our great immortality !
Thick-clustering orbs, and this our fair do-
    main,
The tall, dark mountains, and the deep-toned
    seas
Join in this solemn, universal song.
                Richard Henry Dana.

    The highest, truest thought of heaven which man can have is of the full completion of those processes whose beginnings he has witnessed here, — their completion into degrees of perfectness as yet inconceivable, but still one in kind with what he is aware of now.
                Phillips Brooks.

December 24

We cannot see our Lord unless we die;
This mortal must take immortality.
To that far country He has gone away,
But bade us follow thither day by day.

One moment! then shall I be changed, and
    see
My Lord, turning with love to look on me?
Now sinful, all afraid, with vision dim,
Shall I awake in heaven beholding Him?

Ye angels! roll for me the stone away,
My sepulchre hath light and joy to-day.
His Spirit softly whispers, passing by,
Ye cannot see your Lord unless ye die.

December 25

Peace beginning to be,
Deep as the sleep of the sea
When the stars their faces glass
In its blue tranquillity;
Hearts of men upon earth,
Never once still from their birth,
To rest as the wild waters rest,
With the colors of heaven on their breast.

Love which is sunlight of peace,
Age by age to increase
Till anger and hatred are dead,
And sorrow and death shall cease,
" Peace on earth and good will," —
Souls that are gentle and still
Hear the first music of this
Far-off, infinite bliss.

Edwin Arnold.

December 26

Life is life forever! To be is eternal being. Every man that has died is at this instant in full possession of all his faculties, in
the intensest exercise of all his capacities,
standing somewhere in God's great universe,
ringed with a sense of God's presence, and
feeling in every fibre of his being that life
which comes after death is not less real but
more real, not less great but more great, not
less full or intense but more full and intense,
than the mingled life which, lived here on
earth, was a centre of life surrounded with a
crust and circumstance of mortality. The
dead are the living. They lived while they
died, and after they die they live on forever.

Alexander Maclaren.

December 27

Do you go to your graves these winter days, and observe how the flowers you tended there last summer are dead, and think of other and fairer dead, of which those were but the poor imitation? For the sake of all that can fill you with the everlasting life, open your heart to the sense of that spring-tide sure to rise when the sun comes back, and tell your soul that is but the intimation also of the spring-tide poor David Gray sang about, as he lay a-dying, in the first bloom of his life : —

> "There is life with God
> In other kingdoms of a sweeter air :
> In Eden every flower is blown. — Amen."

So may all sing, if to an inreaching faith they will add an outlooking hope, — will know that this fluttering of the heart, that causes them to open their eyes wide, reaches for its fruition into certainties immutable as heaven. — *Robert Collyer*.

December 28

The " dead " and the " living " are not names of two classes which exclude each other. Much rather there are none who are dead. The dead are simply the living who have died. While they were dying they lived, and after they were dead they lived more fully. All live unto God. " God is not the God of the dead, but of the living."

Alexander Maclaren.

All things around us and in us are felt to be beginnings ; and the curtains of the unseen world, as if lifted by the wind, wave ever and anon into our face, and cling to it like a mask we see through, or think we see. . . . Neither can we resist the conviction that this world is for us only the porch of another and more magnificent temple of the Creator's majesty, wherein we shall enter still further into the Creator's power, and learn that to be in the Creator's power is the creature's happiness.

F. W. Faber.

December 29

Death is not death if it takes away from that mother forever all a mother's anxieties, a mother's fears, and lets her see, in the gracious countenance of her Saviour, a sure and certain pledge that those she has left behind are safe, safe with Christ and in Christ, through all the chances and dangers of this mortal life.

Charles Kingsley.

The tree that waves its branches so freely in the great expanse, and spreads out its leafy surface toward heaven, so eager for light and heat, struck its root in secret, under ground, in great darkness and bondage. Take heed that you do not undervalue your time of spiritual darkness and conflict. The joy of eternity often strikes its root in very bitterness of spirit. Do you know that you would not so painfully feel your darkness if the holy sunlight did not underlie it? The diviner the sunlight at the centre, the painfuller is the encompassing night. — *John Pulsford.*

December 30

How wonderful is sudden death if we think rightly of it! One moment speaking with friends on the earth, and the next in the sudden intuition of the heavenly language with saints in heaven! One moment treading the stony paths of the city street, the next the golden pavement of the new Jerusalem! One moment here on the earth in faintness and sudden prostration of power, the next in fullness of immortal youth, of immortal and glorious peace and power! One moment seeing the Master through the Gospel, through worship and sacrament, and yet as through a glass darkly, and then face to face!

No, we need not mourn for those suddenly called, as if it were a disaster; for it is to them a superlative victory, a sudden flash of radiant glory, an instantaneous coronation.

R. S. Storrs, D. D.

December 31

Why cry so many voices choked with tears,
" The year is dead " ? It rather seems to me
Full of such rich and boundless life to be,
It is a presage of the eternal years.

Must it not live in us while we, too, live ?
Part of ourselves are now the joys it brought ;
Part of ourselves, too, is the good it wrought
In days of darkness.   Years to come may
       give
Less conflict, less of pain, less doubt, dismay,
A larger share of brightness than this last ;
But victory won in darkness that is past
Is a possession that will far outweigh
All we have lost.   So let us rather cry,
This year of grace still lives : it cannot die !
Mary G. Slocum.

As narrower grows the earthly chain,
The circle widens in the sky;
These are our treasures that remain,
But those are stars that beam on high.

HOLMES.

January

February

March

April

May

June

July

August

September

October

November

December

The Riverside Press

CAMBRIDGE, MASSACHUSETTS, U. S. A
ELECTROTYPED AND PRINTED BY
H. O. HOUGHTON AND CO.

CPSIA information can be obtained at www.ICGtesting.com
Printed in the USA
BVOW09s1310060215

386697BV00014B/131/P